80 SLURPABLE NOODLE RECIPES FROM ASIA

Smith
Street
Books

10
STIR-FRIED

46
SOUP

82
CHILLED

106
INSTANT

126
BASICS

INTRODUCTION

Humans have been slurping noodles for thousands of years. Within that span, we've stretched, pulled and cut basic ingredients, such as wheat, rice and eggs into a dizzying array of long, short, fat, thin, fresh and dried noods, all dictated by local knowledge, tradition, geography and midnight cravings.

Most likely, noodles were invented in China, centuries before the rise of pasta around the Mediterranean. Since their nascence, they've taken centre stage in national dishes and they get university students through the years of shallower pockets. Flash-fried into crinkling, shiny packages or twisted and folded by the hands of masters, the world of noodles encompasses hundreds of dishes and budgets, from bowls fit for a wedding to cheese melted and mixed into the sweet, sweet MSG of a flavour packet.

This book is a small slice of a wide world, full of recipes from a collection of chefs. These dishes' origins are scattered throughout Asia and include China, Japan, Korea, Vietnam, Thailand and Malaysia. Food borders are amorphous, and some of these dishes are shared among multiple countries with a common noodle heritage; others have a hometown and specific story that brought them to our tables. All of them are delicious.

When the days get colder, the Soup chapter has bowls to lift your spirits – a Tantanmen (page 56) if you're craving something spicy, or *Lẩu* (Vietnamese Hotpot; page 76) to gather round with friends. Start your day off right with the Stir-fried chapter and whip up some *Re gan mian* (Hot dry noodles; page 24) or end a night out with a beer and *Pad kee mao* (Thai drunken noodles; page 35). If the summertime heat's too much to be bothered, the Chilled chapter's *Zaru soba* (Chilled soba; page 90) or *Bún thịt nướng* (Grilled pork and vermicelli noodle salad; page 103) might be just the thing. And if you're on a budget, short on time or just have a craving, check out the Instant chapter for Tomato egg noodles (page 108) and a *Gong zai mein* (HK breakfast; page 113).

Noods invites you to slurp your way through these recipes and many more. Stock up on noodles and visit old favourites, discover new staples and enjoy a umami-filled exploration of your local Asian grocer.

NOOODLE ESSENTIALS

When in doubt, just head to your local Asian supermarket for these ingredients.

BELACAN
This staple of Peranakan and Malay cuisine is made from krill (tiny shrimp-like crustaceans) that have been salted, dried and fermented, which yields its deep salty-umami. Toast raw *belacan* in a dry frying pan before using for best results.

BONITO FLAKES
The bonito tuna is dried and then shaved, producing flakes that are smoky, savoury and a staple of Japanese cuisine. Add it to dishes or sprinkle it on top as a garnish and watch it dance.

CHINESE BLACK VINEGAR
Fermented rice produces this vingear whose appearance lives up to its name. Black in colour, it's unique in smell and flavour. Slightly sweeter than other vinegars, it has a malty taste and appears throughout Chinese cooking.

CHINESE SESAME PASTE
Though it's also made from sesame seeds, this paste is much thicker than tahini. The seeds are toasted, which create the paste's nutty, aromatic quality.

DOUBANJIANG
A paste commonly used in Chinese dishes. It's made with fermented soybeans, broad beans and chilli. Some versions are spicy. Some are not. Any version will make your food absolutely delicious.

DRIED SHRIMP
Common across Asian cuisines, sun-dried shrimp are popular for their unique taste that packs a sweet umami. Shrunk to the size of a thumbnail, their flavour is a whole lot larger.

FERMENTED SOYBEAN SAUCE
Tao jeow adds a salty kick to dishes. Also known as yellow bean paste, this Thai condiment is made from soybeans that are salted and left to ferment.

GOCHUGARU

These Korean chilli flakes (also called Korean chilli powder), are widely used in Korean dishes. *Gochugaru* usually comes in two forms: coarse chilli flakes or fine powder.

GOCHUJANG

Gochujang is a spicy-sweet fermented chilli paste widely used in Korean cuisine. Try it once and you'll keep it stocked in your fridge forever.

MIRIN

A rice wine common in Japanese cooking, with an alcohol content lower than sake's. Mirin brings a sweeter note to dishes with a subtle hit of tang.

MUSTARD GREENS

Two types of preserved mustard greens appear in this book: *suimiyacai* (pickled and dried mustard greens) and *zah cai* (pickled mustard greens). Both are made from the plant's stem. The first is popular in Sichuan cuisine and adds a salty crunch to dishes, used here in Dan Dan Noodles (page 14). The second tastes similar but has a stronger flavour that packs a lot of zing in a little bite.

SHAOXING RICE WINE

This rice wine is key to Chinese cooking, used in dishes ranging from soups to wontons. It adds a complexity to dishes, introducing a rich, nutty flavour that creates a rich depth in anything you add it to.

SHICHIMI TOGARASHI

A Japanese spice mixture containing seven ingredients – red chilli pepper, sansho pepper, hemp seeds and/or poppy seeds, sesame seeds, ginger, citrus peel and nori. It's a welcome seasoning on ramen or rice dishes (or anything else you're inspired to sprinkle it on).

TAMARIND

Used dried, as a sauce, or in a paste: the pulp from the tamarind fruit has many purposes. It's popular across Asian cuisines for the sour and sweet to tangy and tart flavours it can add to a dish.

NOODLE ESSENTIALS

CANTONESE CHOW MEIN

If you've eaten Chinese food in the West, chances are, chow mein has appeared on your plate. This particular version, however, is less well known outside of China – Cantonese chow mein's noodles are crispier and drier. It's a simple side dish that lets soy sauce's umami really shine.

SERVES 4

350 g (12½ oz) pan-fried thin noodles (see Note)

3 tbsp vegetable oil

½ onion, finely sliced

3 spring (green) onions, white and green parts separated, cut into 5 cm (2 in) lengths

100 g (3½ oz) bean sprouts

2 tsp sesame oil

1 tsp toasted sesame seeds, to garnish

SAUCE

½ tbsp dark soy sauce

1 tbsp light soy sauce

1 tbsp oyster sauce

2 tsp granulated sugar

2 tbsp water

Place 500 ml (2 cups) of water in a non-stick wok and bring to the boil over high heat. Place the noodles on a steamer rack and lower it into the wok. Cover with a lid, increase the heat to medium–high and steam the noodles for 5 minutes.

Meanwhile, mix all of the sauce ingredients together in a small bowl, adjusting for taste, and set aside.

When the noodles have finished steaming – they should be a translucent yellow – turn the heat off. Remove the steamer from the wok and drop the noodles into the hot water. Give them a quick stir for 15 seconds to loosen them up, then drain them, shake off any excess water and set aside.

Heat 1 tablespoon of the oil in the cleaned wok or a frying pan over medium–high heat. Add the onion and white parts of the spring onion, stir-fry for a minute, then remove from the wok and set aside.

In the same wok, heat another tablespoon of oil over medium–low heat. Add the noodles and spread them out evenly with chopsticks. Do not stir – let them gently fry until lightly golden and crispy, about 3 minutes. Then flip the noodles, drizzle another tablespoon of oil over them and gently fry for another 3 minutes. Gently move the noodles with chopsticks occasionally to keep them loose.

Move the noodles to one side of the wok, add the bean sprouts and give them a quick stir-fry. Flip the noodles over the sprouts and cook for 30 seconds. Add both the cooked and remaining onions, pour the sauce over the noodles and stir-fry everything for 2 minutes until all the sauce has been soaked up by the noodles. Taste and adjust the seasoning as needed.

Drizzle with sesame oil and give the noodles a quick toss for 10 seconds, then divide among serving bowls. Sprinkle with sesame seeds and serve.

NOTE: The noodles in this recipe are precooked and coated in oil. Alternatively, you can use fresh wonton egg noodles and prepare them according to the packet instructions.

DAN DAN MIAN

A Sichuan classic beloved by many, for good reason – noodles doused in a spicy sauce that are easy to make but hard to stop slurping. Dan dan noodles' flavour comes, in part, from *suimiyacai* (pickled and dried mustard greens) and Sichuan peppercorns, which are both common in the region's cooking.

SERVES 2

1 tbsp vegetable oil

1 star anise

250 g (9 oz) minced (ground) pork

15 g (½ oz) ginger, finely chopped

50 g (1¾ oz) suimiyacai preserved vegetables

2 tbsp light soy sauce

1 tbsp dark soy sauce

450 g (1 lb) fresh Shanghai noodles

1 bunch baby bok choy (pak choy), quartered lengthwise

2 spring (green) onions, finely sliced

40 g (1½ oz) Roasted peanuts (see page 133)

SAUCE

2 tbsp light soy sauce

1 tbsp dark soy sauce

2 tsp Chinese black vinegar

2 tsp Chinese sesame paste

1 tsp Sichuan peppercorn powder (see Note)

1 tsp red chilli oil

Heat the oil and star anise in a wok over high heat. Once smoking, add the minced pork, ginger and suimiyacai, stir-frying until all the juice has evaporated, about 2 minutes. Add the light and dark soy sauce, and stir-fry until the pork is nicely browned, another minute. Turn off the heat, transfer the pork to a heatproof bowl, remove the star anise and discard.

To make the sauce, place all of the ingredients in a large mixing bowl and stir until combined.

Bring a medium saucepan of water to a rolling boil over high heat. Once boiling, add the noodles and cook for 2 minutes. While the noodles are cooking, blanch the bok choy for 30 seconds, then remove and set them aside. Strain the noodles, reserving the cooking water, and transfer the noodles to the mixing bowl with the sauce. Stir until all the noodles are well coated in the chilli sauce, adding 250 ml (1 cup) of the cooking water if the noodles are dry.

Divide the noodles between serving bowls, top with the bok choy and pork, then garnish with spring onion and roasted peanuts.

NOTE: You can find Sichuan peppercorn powder at Asian supermarkets. Alternatively, you can make your own by toasting Sichuan peppercorns lightly, then grinding them using a mortar and pestle.

Tender, marinated slices of beef, tossed with rice noodles make this Cantonese dish a favourite among noodle lovers. Traditionally stir-fried in a wok, Beef *chow fun* is very quick to cook. This recipe is made to share, but if you eat the whole thing yourself, we won't tell.

SERVES 2

250 g (9 oz) flank or skirt steak

340 g (12 oz) fresh flat rice noodles (see Note)

3 tbsp vegetable oil

½ onion, finely sliced

3 spring (green) onions, white and green parts separated, cut into 5 cm (2 in) lengths and white parts sliced in half

1 tbsp light soy sauce

½ tbsp dark soy sauce

½ tbsp oyster sauce

1 tsp sesame oil

90 g (1 cup) bean sprouts

2 tsp toasted sesame seeds, to garnish

Sichuan crispy chilli oil, to serve (see page 133)

BEEF MARINADE

½ tsp baking soda

½ tbsp cornflour (cornstarch)

½ tbsp oyster sauce

½ tbsp light soy sauce

1 tsp dark soy sauce

½ tsp ground white pepper

1 tsp Shaoxing rice wine

1 tsp granulated sugar

Place the steak in the freezer for 30 minutes until slightly frozen, then cut the meat against the grain into slices 3 mm (⅛ in) thick. Place the beef slices in a bowl, then cover with room-temperature water and soak for 10 minutes.

Prepare the beef marinade by mixing all the ingredients together in a medium bowl.

Drain the beef and squeeze out all the excess water. Add the beef to the marinade, mixing with your hands until well coated. Set aside to marinate.

Separate the noodles. If they are stiff, place them in the microwave for 30 seconds to loosen, then gently pull them apart. Repeat until all the noodles are separated, place in a bowl and set aside.

When ready to stir-fry, add 1 tablespoon of the oil to the beef mixture and stir to mix well.

Heat the remaining oil in a wok over high heat until it starts to ripple. Add the beef mixture, spreading the pieces out and cooking for 20 seconds, then stir-frying until the beef is cooked but still lightly pink, about 30 seconds. Remove the beef and set aside, drain all the excess oil, reserving 1 tablespoon, and wipe the wok clean.

Return the reserved oil to the wok and heat again over medium–high heat. Add the onion and spring onion (white part) and stir-fry until fragrant, about 20 seconds. Add the noodles, and using tongs or chopsticks, stir-fry them gently until slightly charred, about 2 minutes. Add the soy and oyster sauces and sesame oil and stir-fry for 30 seconds until the noodles are well coated.

Add the beef to the noodles and toss the wok for 30 seconds to mix everything together. Turn off the heat and add the spring onion (green part) and bean sprouts, quickly tossing. Divide between serving bowls, sprinkle with sesame seeds and serve with chilli oil on the side.

NOTE: Fresh flat rice noodles usually come congealed in a block and are stored in the fridge. If using dry flat rice noodles instead, soak the noodles in hot water according to the packet instructions.

BEEF CHOW FUN

At first glance, Shanghai fried noodles may look like other stir-fries, but this dish is set apart by its star – thick, chewy noodles. A quick, easy meal, with a mix of pork and vegetables that's as delicious as it is simple.

SERVES 2

250 g (9 oz) pork loin, cut into thin strips

1 tbsp vegetable oil

3 fresh shiitake mushrooms, finely sliced

100 g (3½ oz) cabbage, cut into 1 cm (½ in) strips

1 carrot, julienned

3 garlic cloves, finely chopped

200 ml (7 fl oz) water

250 g (9 oz) Shanghai thick yellow noodles (see Note)

MARINADE

2 tsp light soy sauce

1 tsp ground white pepper

1 tsp caster (superfine) sugar

2 tsp cornflour (cornstarch)

2 tsp Shaoxing rice wine

2 tsp vegetable oil

SAUCE

1 tbsp oyster sauce

2 tbsp light soy sauce

2 tbsp dark soy sauce

1 tsp caster sugar

Place the pork strips and all the marinade ingredients except the oil in a mixing bowl. Stir everything together with your hands to mix well. Add the oil and massage for another 10 seconds, set aside and let marinate for a minute.

To make the sauce, place all the ingredients into a small bowl and stir to mix well.

Heat the oil in a wok over high heat until smoking and add the pork strips, spread out, reserving the marinade. Cook for 30 seconds without stirring. Flip the pork strips over and stir-fry for a minute. Add the mushrooms and stir-fry for 30 seconds. Add the cabbage, carrot and garlic and stir to mix well. Add the water and the sauce, give it a quick stir and wait until the water is bubbling. Add the noodles and stir until they are well coated, then cover with a lid, reduce the heat to low and cook for 1–3 minutes. Remove the lid and give the noodles a stir. If there is still a lot of liquid in the wok, turn the heat to medium and continue stir-frying until most of the sauce has evaporated. Divide between serving bowls and serve immediately.

NOTE: Shanghai thick yellow noodles usually come precooked – all you have to do is reheat them and they're ready to eat. If using fresh noodles, prepare the noodles by halving the cooking time, according to the packet instructions. Alternatively, you can use udon noodles instead.

ZHA JIANG MIAN

Zha jiang mian, or Fried sauce noodles, is a signature dish from Beijing's kitchens. If you'd like to experience the city's cuisine, these noodles are a slightly cheaper and quicker route than Peking duck. Made with ground pork, vegetables and a rich, fragrant sauce, it's a classic for a reason.

SERVES 4

2 tbsp vegetable oil

350 g (12½ oz) minced (ground) pork (70% lean, 30% fat)

1 tbsp liaojiu cooking wine (see Note)

5 cm (2 in) piece ginger, finely grated

3 spring (green) onions, white parts only, finely chopped

3 garlic cloves, minced

2 tbsp spicy doubanjiang sauce

125 ml (½ cup) water

2 tbsp sweet tianmianjiang sauce (see Note)

350 g (12½ oz) fresh wheat noodles (see Note)

2 carrots, julienned

1 short cucumber, julienned

Heat the oil in a wok over medium–high heat until it starts to ripple. Add the minced pork and stir-fry until browned, about 2 minutes. Add the cooking wine and stir-fry until all the liquid has evaporated, about 30 seconds. Add the ginger, spring onions and garlic and stir-fry until fragrant, about a minute.

Add the doubanjiang sauce and water, stirring to mix well. Add the tianmianjiang sauce and stir to combine. Reduce the heat to low and simmer until the sauce thickens and becomes darker in colour, about 5 minutes.

Meanwhile, bring a medium saucepan of water to a rolling boil over high heat. Cook the noodles for 2 minutes, stirring occasionally. Drain the noodles, then run them under cold water for 30 seconds. Shake off excess water, and divide the noodles equally among serving bowls.

Place a handful of the carrot and cucumber in each bowl, then pour a ladleful of the pork mixture over the noodles and serve.

NOTE: *Liaojiu* is a cooking rice wine, widely used in Chinese cooking to reduce or eliminate the strong smell and flavour of meat like beef or pork. Alternatively, you can substitute Shaoxing rice wine.

Tianmianjiang is a thick, brown sauce made from wheat flour and sometimes fermented soybeans. The sauce has a savoury sweet and salty profile, which adds umami to the dish.

In this recipe, we used fresh thick wheat noodles that have a nice chewy texture. Alternatively, you can use udon noodles.

Before you head to the backyard with a bug catcher, there are no actual ants in this dish. Its name (Ants climbing a tree) evokes the way the pork clings to the noodles. Whether or not you like imagining ants in your food, this dish is classically Sichuan – deliciously spicy.

SERVES 4

200 g (7 oz) sweet potato starch noodles (see Note)

10 g (¼ oz) dried wood ear fungus

½ tbsp dark soy sauce

3 tbsp vegetable oil

250 g (9 oz) minced (ground) pork

1 tbsp Shaoxing rice wine

2 spring (green) onions, white and green parts separated, finely sliced

1 cm (½ in) piece ginger, finely chopped

1 tbsp spicy doubanjiang sauce

1 tbsp light soy sauce

1 tsp salt

1 tsp ground white pepper

1 tsp chicken bouillon

1 tbsp oyster sauce

Boil a kettle of water. Place the noodles in a large heatproof bowl, pour hot water over the noodles and soak until softened, about 20 minutes.

Place the wood ear in a small heatproof bowl and add hot water, letting it soak until rehydrated, about 10 minutes. Drain then roughly chop the wood ear into a mince and set aside.

Drain the noodles and shake off any excess water. Place them back into the large bowl, and add the dark soy sauce, stirring until mixed well. Add 1 tablespoon of the oil and stir until the noodles are well coated.

Heat the remaining oil in a wok over medium–high heat, add the pork and stir-fry until cooked, about 2 minutes. Add the rice wine and cook until all the juice has evaporated. Add the spring onion (white part) and ginger, stir-frying for 10 seconds, then add the doubanjiang and the light soy sauce and stir-fry for another 20 seconds. Add the noodles and wood ear, stir-frying until well combined. Reduce the heat to low, season with the salt, pepper, chicken bouillon and oyster sauce, and stir-fry to mix well. Turn off the heat and add the spring onion (green part) and give it a quick stir. Divide among serving bowls.

NOTE: Sweet potato starch noodles are also known as glass noodles. These are the same noodles used for *Japchae* (see page 30). Look for *dangmyeon* noodles at Asian supermarkets.

RE GAN MIAN

Hot dry noodles is a breakfast dish of choice from Wuhan. As its name suggests, it is served without broth. It is not, however, spicy (unless you pile on the chilli oil). The dish is served hot, with a chew to the alkaline noodles and a bite from the spring onions that has made it a favourite throughout China.

SERVES 2

280 g (10 oz) fresh alkaline noodles (see Note)

2 tsp sesame oil

50 g (1¾ oz) preserved mustard greens, shredded (see Note)

2 spring (green) onions, green parts only, finely sliced

50 g (1¾ oz) pickled long beans (see Note)

a handful coriander (cilantro) leaves, roughly chopped, to garnish

Chinese black vinegar, to taste

Sichuan crispy chilli oil, to taste (optional) (see page 133)

DRESSING

2 tbsp sesame paste (see Note)

1 tbsp sesame oil (see Note)

1 tbsp light soy sauce

2 tsp dark soy sauce

2 tbsp water

1 tsp granulated sugar

Prepare a large mixing bowl of iced water and set aside.

Bring a large saucepan of water to a rolling boil, add the noodles, stir and cook according to the packet instructions. Drain and drop the noodles in the iced water. After a few minutes, drain and shake well. Put the noodles in a bowl, add the sesame oil, toss well and set aside.

Next make the dressing. Place all the ingredients except the water in a bowl, and stir until it becomes a thick paste. Add a tablespoon of water at a time, and stir until it has a pouring consistency.

When ready to serve, bring a saucepan of water to a rolling boil. Place half of the noodles in a mesh strainer and lower it into the hot water, stirring the noodles with chopsticks for 10 seconds before lifting them out and shaking off any excess water. Put the noodles in a serving bowl, then repeat for the second portion of noodles.

Divide the mustard greens, spring onion and pickled long beans equally between the serving bowls. Garnish with coriander, add 2 tablespoons of the dressing and a dash of black vinegar.

Serve the noodles sprinkled with chilli oil, if using.

NOTE: Alkaline noodles are wheat noodles with a higher quantity of alkali, which gives the noodles a distinctively springy, chewy mouth-feel. In this recipe, you can substitute fresh Chinese *lamian* or fresh Japanese ramen noodles, but not the dry versions.

The preserved mustard greens can be substituted with pickled chilli radish.

Pickled long beans are available at Asian supermarkets.

Instead of using sesame paste and oil, you can substitute tahini, which already has a pouring consistency.

SINGAPORE MEI FUN

These noodles are not, in fact, from Singapore. If you search for them there, you'll have a hard time, as they are actually from Hong Kong. A dish that's easy to whip up in minutes, Singapore noodles are easy to adjust to your taste or whatever ingredients you might have in the fridge.

SERVES 2

200 g (7 oz) dried rice vermicelli

3 tbsp vegetable oil

2 garlic cloves, finely chopped

2 shallots, diced

1–2 fresh red chillies, deseeded and finely sliced

80 g (2¾ oz) boneless, skinless chicken breast, cut into thin strips

200 g (7 oz) medium-sized fresh prawns (shrimp), peeled and deveined, tails intact

50 g (1¾ oz) cabbage, julienned

20 g (¾ oz) carrot, julienned

2 medium-sized eggs

1 tbsp oyster sauce

¼ tsp ground white pepper, or to taste

¼ tsp salt, or to taste

50 g (1¾ oz) bean sprouts

10 g (¼ oz) spring (green) onions, finely chopped

Soak the rice vermicelli in warm water for 20–30 minutes until softened, then drain and set aside.

Heat 2 tablespoons of the oil in a non-stick frying pan or wok over high heat and then sauté the garlic, shallot and chilli until aromatic. Add the chicken and prawns, then stir-fry until they are cooked, roughly 1–2 minutes. Next add the cabbage and carrot and stir-fry for another minute or until the vegetables have softened.

Push all the ingredients to the side of the wok and then add the remaining tablespoon of oil. Crack the eggs into the space created and allow to cook, undisturbed, until half set. Using a spatula or wooden spoon, scramble the eggs together and fry until golden, then incorporate into the noodles.

Add the oyster sauce, white pepper, salt and vermicelli, then fold until everything is combined. Add the bean sprouts and continue to stir-fry until aromatic.

Turn off the heat and garnish the noodles with spring onion. Serve immediately.

Yakisoba can be found at Japanese food stalls, but you won't find it made with buckwheat noodles. This dish is stir-fried, instead, with wheat-based noodles, cooked with thin cuts of meat, vegetables and a distinct sauce that's both sweet and savoury.

SERVES 4

480 g (1 lb 1 oz) fresh yakisoba noodles (see Note)

2 tbsp vegetable oil

250 g (9 oz) pork belly, thinly sliced

½ onion, finely sliced

1 carrot, finely sliced

3 cabbage leaves, cut into bite-sized pieces (about 1 cup)

5 shiitake mushrooms, finely sliced

2 spring (green) onions, cut into 5 cm (2 in) lengths

freshly ground black pepper, to taste

2 tbsp aonori dried seaweed flakes, to garnish

2 tbsp pickled red ginger, to garnish

SAUCE

60 ml (¼ cup) Japanese Worcestershire sauce (see Note)

1 tbsp oyster sauce

1 tbsp ketchup

2 tsp light soy sauce

2 tsp caster (superfine) sugar

Rinse the noodles under running room-temperature water. Use your hands to gently loosen and separate the noodles. Drain well and shake off as much water as possible. Place in a bowl and set aside.

To make the sauce, whisk all the ingredients in a mixing bowl until combined and the sugar has dissolved. Taste and adjust accordingly.

Heat 1 tablespoon of the oil in a non-stick frying pan or wok over medium–high heat. Add the noodles and spread them out evenly with chopsticks. Do not stir – let them gently fry until lightly golden and crispy, about 3 minutes. Then flip the noodles, drizzle another tablespoon of oil over them and gently fry undisturbed for another 2 minutes. Transfer the noodles to a large plate.

In the same pan, heat the remaining oil over medium–high heat and cook the pork belly until caramelised on the edges, about 3 minutes. Add the onions and carrot, stir-frying for 2 minutes until the onions are translucent. Add the cabbage and cook until softened, about 3 minutes. Add the mushrooms and spring onions, stir-fry for another minute, then add the noodles, 125 ml (½ cup) of the sauce and black pepper, stir-frying until the noodles are well coated, around 3 minutes. Taste and add more sauce if needed, cooking until the sauce has evaporated.

Divide the noodles among serving bowls, and garnish with aonori and pickled red ginger to serve.

NOTE: Fresh pre-steamed yakisoba noodles are widely available in Japanese and Asian supermarkets, sometimes even in standard supermarkets. You can also use dried yakisoba noodles, prepared according to the instructions on the packet.

Japanese Worcestershire sauce is usually sweeter and less sour than the English version. The most commonly used is Bull-Dog brand.

JAPCHAE

No introduction to Korean food would be complete without *Japchae*. It's one of the most popular noodle dishes in its home country, created by mixing sweet potato starch noodles, vegetables and *bulgogi* (soy-marinated barbecued beef). Toss them together and you have a perfect blend of textures. Serve as a side with other Korean dishes, or with rice to make it a complete meal.

SERVES 4

170 g (6 oz) sweet potato starch noodles

vegetable oil, for frying

1 egg

1 onion, finely sliced

1 spring (green) onion, cut into 5 cm (2 in) lengths

1 medium carrot, julienned

4–5 dried shiitake mushrooms, soaked in warm water for 2–3 hours, cut into strips

110 g (4 oz) Bulgogi (Soy-marinated barbecued beef) (see page 129), uncooked

½ quantity Sigeumchi muchim (Seasoned english spinach) (see page 132)

DRESSING

60 ml (¼ cup) soy sauce

1 tbsp caster (superfine) sugar

2 tbsp sesame oil

2 garlic cloves, grated

2 tsp toasted sesame seeds

To make the dressing, whisk together all the ingredients in a small bowl until the sugar has dissolved.

Cut the sweet potato starch noodles in half using a pair of kitchen scissors. Bring a saucepan of water to a rolling boil over high heat. Add the noodles and cook according to the packet instructions until soft and chewy. Drain the noodles and rinse under cold running water until chilled. Combine the noodles with 2 tablespoons of the dressing in a large bowl and mix well.

Heat 1 tablespoon of vegetable oil in a large non-stick frying pan or wok over medium heat. Add the noodles and stir-fry for 3–4 minutes until the noodles are translucent. Return the noodles to the bowl.

Crack the egg into a small bowl and lightly beat with a fork. Heat 1 tablespoon of oil over medium heat in a separate pan. Pour in the beaten egg, swirl to spread evenly and cook until the surface is almost set, about 1 minute. Flip the egg over and cook the other side, about 30 seconds. Transfer to a chopping board and let it cool. Cut egg into 5cm (2 in) strips, stack them up, then cut into thin strips and set aside.

In the pan you cooked the noodles in, heat another tablespoon of oil, add the onion and spring onion and stir-fry for 1 minute, until the onion is a little translucent. Add the carrot and stir-fry for another minute, then transfer to the bowl with the noodles.

Add 1–2 teaspoons of oil to the same pan, add the mushrooms and bulgogi, and stir-fry for 2–3 minutes until the beef has browned. Add to the noodles.

Add the seasoned spinach to the noodle bowl, pour over the remaining dressing, and toss everything together with your hands. Taste and adjust the seasoning accordingly. Pile onto a large serving plate and serve warm.

P A D   T H A I

Is it possible to think of Thai food without Pad thai? That tang of lime, that crunch of peanuts, the mouth-watering sauce ... It's a truly hard-hitting plate of food gifted to the world by Central Thailand. Much could be said about the dish, but we'll let this recipe speak for itself.

SERVES 2

50 g (1¾ oz) dried thin, flat rice noodles

80 ml (⅓ cup) vegetable oil

300 g (10½ oz) fresh banana prawns (shrimp), peeled and deveined, tails intact

120 g (4 oz) firm tofu, cut into 2 cm × 1 cm (¾ in × ½ in) pieces

90 g (1 cup) bean sprouts

2 eggs (preferably duck eggs if you have them)

25 g (1 oz) garlic chives, cut into 5 cm (2 in) lengths, plus extra to serve

30 g (1 oz) dried shrimp

3 tbsp chopped pickled turnip

2 lime wedges, to serve

PAD THAI SAUCE

3 tbsp tamarind sauce

35 g (1¼ oz) coconut sugar

2 tbsp fish sauce

Fill a large bowl with cold water and soak the noodles until softened, about 20–30 minutes. Drain and set aside.

To make the pad thai sauce, combine all the ingredients in a non-reactive bowl, mix well and set aside.

Heat the oil in a wok over medium–high heat and stir-fry the prawns for 2 minutes, or until golden and just cooked. Remove from the oil with a slotted spoon and set aside to drain on paper towel. Add the tofu to the wok and stir-fry until golden, then add the bean sprouts and stir-fry for 2 minutes. Pour in the pad thai sauce, followed by the noodles. Stir vigorously to mix well.

Move the noodles to one side of the wok. Crack the eggs into the space created and allow to cook, undisturbed, until half set. Using a spatula or wooden spoon, scramble the eggs together and fry until golden, then incorporate into the noodles. Add the prawns, garlic chives, dried shrimp and pickled turnip and stir for 30 seconds, then remove from the heat.

Divide the pad thai between two plates and serve garnished with the lime wedges and extra garlic chives.

Drinking is not a requirement to enjoy Thai drunken noodles, but an ice-cold beer is a great way to wash it down. The spice from the chillies and the freshness of the basil give this Thai street-food favourite its place in the noodle hall of fame.

SERVES 2

340 g (12 oz) fresh flat rice noodles (see Note)

2 tbsp vegetable oil

2 tbsp finely chopped garlic (about 8 cloves)

5 bird's eye chillies, finely sliced (see Note)

1 small shallot, finely sliced

230 g (8 oz) large fresh prawns (shrimp), peeled and deveined, tails intact

2 bunches (150 g/5½ oz) Chinese broccoli (gai lan), cut into bite-sized pieces

1 large red chilli, finely sliced on the diagonal

2 young peppercorn stems (optional) (see Note)

30 g (1 cup) sweet basil leaves

SAUCE

2 tbsp oyster sauce

1 tbsp fish sauce

1 tbsp light soy sauce

½ tbsp dark soy sauce

1 tbsp granulated sugar

pinch of ground white pepper

Boil a kettle of water. Place the noodles in a large heatproof bowl, pour hot water over them and soak for 20 seconds. Drain and let cool, loosening the noodles with your hands if they are stuck in big clumps. Alternatively, place the noodles in the microwave for 20 seconds, then gently pull them apart. Repeat until all the noodles are separated, place in a bowl and set aside.

To make the sauce, combine all the ingredients in a small bowl and adjust to taste.

Heat the oil in a wok over high heat until smoking hot. Add the garlic, bird's eye chillies and shallot and stir-fry for 10 seconds. Add the prawns and stir-fry until just cooked, about 2 minutes. Add the noodles and the sauce and stir-fry, being gentle with the noodles, for another minute until all the sauce has been soaked up by the noodles. Add the Chinese broccoli, large red chilli slices, peppercorn stems, if using, and basil, and cook for another minute, stirring occasionally, then serve.

NOTE: Fresh noodles usually come congealed in a block and are stored in the fridge. You can use dry rice noodles instead, if you like – prepare them according to the packet instructions. You can even use spaghetti!

Bird's eye chillies are very hot, please adjust the level of heat according to taste.

Young green peppercorn stems can be found at Asian supermarkets.

P A D
S E E E W

Pad see ew is a Thai dish with Chinese influences. It has cousins in Beef *chow fun* and *Char kuey teow* (pages 17 and 44) – it's also cooked in a wok and uses flat rice noodles. You'll find variations to *Pad see ew* throughout Thailand. This traditional version from Bangkok features pork.

SERVES 2

300 g (10½ oz) pork tenderloin, finely sliced

3 tbsp dark soy sauce

300 g (10½ oz) fresh flat rice noodles

100 ml (3½ fl oz) vegetable oil

1 tbsp minced garlic

2 eggs, beaten

2 tbsp fish sauce

2 tbsp caster (superfine) sugar

1 tbsp fermented soybean sauce (tao jeow)

1 bunch Chinese broccoli (gai lan), finely sliced on the diagonal

pinch of ground white pepper, to taste (optional)

chilli flakes, to taste (optional)

PORK MARINADE

1 tbsp minced garlic

1 tbsp caster (superfine) sugar

1 tbsp tapioca flour

½ tbsp fish sauce

1 tsp ground white pepper

1 tbsp oyster sauce

1 tbsp grapeseed oil

First, marinate the pork. Combine all the marinade ingredients in a large non-reactive bowl and add the sliced pork. Mix well, then cover with plastic wrap and transfer to the fridge to marinate for 1 hour.

In a separate bowl, mix the dark soy sauce and the flat noodles together, separating the noodles as you go. This will prevent the noodles from sticking to each other. Set aside.

Heat the oil in a wok over medium–high heat and stir-fry the garlic until fragrant. Add the marinated pork and stir-fry for 2–3 minutes. Pour in the beaten egg. Stir with a spatula to roughly break it up, then push the egg to the side of the wok and leave to cook until golden.

Add the noodles, fish sauce, sugar and soybean sauce to the wok and stir-fry the until the noodles are coated, taking care to stir continuously to prevent the noodles from sticking together. Add the Chinese broccoli and stir-fry until it softens, then taste the noodles and adjust the seasoning if necessary. Remove from the heat.

Divide the noodles between two plates and sprinkle with white pepper and chilli flakes, if using, before serving.

RAD NA SEN MI

Rice vermicelli in thick gravy is a common combination found among Bangkok's street-food scene. Caramelised with dark soy sauce, the noodles should be quite dry before you drench them in gravy.

SERVES 4

170 g (6 oz) dried rice vermicelli

80 ml (⅓ cup) vegetable oil

80 ml (⅓ cup) dark soy sauce

5 garlic cloves, finely chopped

500 g (1 lb 2 oz) fresh banana prawns (shrimp), peeled and deveined, tails intact

2 bunches Chinese broccoli (gai lan), sliced on the diagonal

1.5 litres (6 cups) pork stock

1 tbsp fermented soybean sauce (tao jeow)

2 tbsp soy sauce

2 tbsp oyster sauce

1 tsp caster (superfine) sugar

75 g (2¾ oz) cornflour (cornstarch)

ground white pepper, to taste

chilli flakes or pickled chillies, to taste

Fill a large bowl with cold water and soak the vermicelli until softened. Drain and set aside for 15 minutes to dry.

Heat 1 tablespoon of the oil in a wok over medium heat and stir-fry the vermicelli and dark soy sauce until the noodles are evenly coated. Transfer the noodles to a bowl and set aside.

Heat the remaining vegetable oil in a clean wok over medium heat and sauté the garlic until fragrant, then add the prawns and stir-fry until coloured all over. Add the Chinese broccoli and stir-fry for 2 minutes, or until wilted, then pour in the stock. Bring to the boil and season with the fermented soybean sauce, soy sauce, oyster sauce and sugar.

In a small bowl, combine the cornflour and 60 ml (¼ cup) of water, stirring until smooth. Slowly drizzle the cornflour mixture into the wok, stirring constantly until the stock thickens.

To serve, divide the vermicelli among four plates and ladle over a generous amount of gravy. Arrange the prawns and Chinese broccoli on top. Season with pepper and chilli flakes or pickled chillies to taste.

You'll find *Hokkien mee* throughout Southeast Asia, and particularly in Malaysia and Singapore. This is the Kuala Lumpur version: thick, chewy noodles, covered in a glossy, perfectly sweet and salty sauce, with bites of juicy prawns and pork belly.

SERVES 2–3

2 tbsp vegetable oil

200 g (7 oz) pork belly, finely sliced

3 garlic cloves, finely chopped

250 g (9 oz) medium-sized fresh prawns (shrimp), peeled and deveined, tails intact

1 small green round cabbage (about 150 g/5½ oz), cut into strips

3 tbsp dark soy sauce

2–3 tbsp sweet soy sauce or kecap manis (see Note)

1 tsp ground white pepper

⅛ tsp salt, or to taste

450 g (1 lb) thick yellow hokkien noodles

crispy pork lard, to serve (optional)

Malaysian chilli paste, to serve (optional) (see page 44)

Heat the oil in a non-stick frying pan or wok over high heat and add the pork belly. Stir-fry until the pork belly has released some fat and is browned on the edges.

Add the garlic and prawns, and stir-fry until the prawns are half cooked, about 1 minute. Then add the cabbage and toss for another 30 seconds.

Add the soy sauces, white pepper and season with salt to taste. Bring to a simmer – if needed, you can add about 60 ml (¼ oup) of water and let the sauce reduce a bit before adding the noodles.

Toss everything together until the noodles are well coated with the sauce, then stir-fry until most of the sauce has evaporated, about 3–4 minutes.

Remove from the heat and divide the noodles among serving bowls. For added flavour, serve with crispy pork lard or Malaysian chilli paste.

NOTE: *Kecap manis* is a popular Indonesian ingredient. With the rich consistency of molasses, it's created with palm sugar and soy sauce, and oan be found in most supermarkets.

MEE GORENG MAMAK

On the streets of Malaysia, hawkers whip up Mamak-style stir-fried noodles in minutes, and you'll often see long lines queuing patiently for this street-food classic. The fried noodles are packed with sweet and spicy flavours, and a nuttiness from the special paste made with dried shrimp and chilli paste.

SERVES 4

100 ml (3½ fl oz) vegetable oil

250 g (9 oz) firm tofu, sliced in half horizontally

3 garlic cloves, grated

2 red shallots, finely sliced

2 small potatoes, peeled, boiled and diced

2 small tomatoes, diced

300 g (10½ oz) yellow noodles, blanched according to the packet instructions

4 small eggs

90 g (1 cup) bean sprouts

MEE GORENG MAMAK PASTE

125 ml (½ cup) vegetable oil

1 tbsp yellow lentils

80 g (1 cup) dried shrimp, soaked in water for 10 minutes, drained

2½ tbsp Malaysian chilli paste (see page 44)

3–4 tbsp sugar

125 g (4½ oz) ground dry-roasted peanuts

1 tbsp tamarind paste

GARNISHES

1 cos (romaine) lettuce, shredded

2 long red chillies, sliced

crispy fried shallots

2 limes, quartered

To make the mee goreng mamak paste, heat the oil in a wok over medium heat and fry the yellow lentils for about 1 minute. Add the dried shrimp and stir until golden brown. Scoop out the lentil and dried shrimp mix using a fine-mesh sieve and reserve the frying oil.

Place the fried lentil mixture, chilli paste and 3–4 tablespoons of the frying oil in a blender or food processor and blend to a smooth paste.

Heat the remaining frying oil in the wok over medium heat and stir-fry the paste for 3–4 minutes until it's aromatic and the oil has separated. Stir in the sugar, then add the ground peanuts, tamarind paste and 500 ml (2 cups) of water and mix together well. Season to taste with salt, then simmer for 8–10 minutes until the sauce has reduced and thickened, and the oil has separated. Remove from the heat and leave to cool to room temperature.

Heat 2 tablespoons of the oil in a frying pan over medium heat. Pat the tofu dry and add to the pan, then cook for 3–4 minutes until golden on both sides. Remove and drain on paper towel, then cut each piece into bite-sized chunks.

Heat the remaining oil in a wok or a non-stick frying pan over medium heat. Add the garlic and shallot and cook until golden and fragrant. Add the tofu, potato and tomato and stir-fry for about 30 seconds until combined.

Add 3–4 tablespoons of the mee goreng mamak paste and stir constantly for another 30 seconds. Add the blanched noodles and toss through. Make a well in the middle of the noodle mixture and crack in the eggs. Let them cook for 30 seconds or so, then break up the eggs using a spatula. Stir again for another 30 seconds to mix everything together. Finally, toss through the bean sprouts.

Divide the fried noodles among serving plates and garnish with the lettuce, chilli, crispy fried shallots and lime quarters. Serve immediately.

CHAR KUEY TEOW

Char kuey teow is reason enough to visit Penang, where hawkers work quickly over high heat to give this dish its distinctive charred flavour. Creating *'wok hei'* (breath of the wok) at home may be a tall order, but it's a dish worth eating again and again while you try.

SERVES 2.

500 g (1 lb 2 oz) fresh kuey teow (flat rice noodles)

80 ml (⅓ cup) vegetable oil

4 garlic cloves, minced

1 lap cheong (Chinese sausage), sliced diagonally

8–10 large fresh banana prawns (shrimp), peeled and deveined, tails intact

2 tbsp light soy sauce

2 tbsp dark soy sauce

1 tbsp oyster sauce

2 eggs (preferably duck eggs if you have them)

180 g (2 cups) bean sprouts

2 small handfuls of garlic chives, cut into 2.5 cm (1 in) lengths

MALAYSIAN CHILLI PASTE

5 long red chillies

5 bird's eye chillies

1 tbsp toasted belacan (shrimp paste)

1 tsp granulated sugar

pinch of salt

juice of ½ lime

To make the chilli paste, use a mortar and pestle to pound all the chillies until they are a coarse paste. Add the belacan, sugar and salt and pound for another minute. Add the lime juice and mix well. Set aside (see Note).

Prepare the rice noodles according to the packet instructions. Loosen the strands so they don't clump together and break when you stir-fry them. Set aside.

Heat a wok over high heat until it becomes a bit smoky. Add the oil, immediately followed by the garlic and 1 tablespoon of the chilli paste and give it a quick stir. Add the lap cheong and stir briefly, then add the prawns and stir with a spatula for 1 minute or just until they turn pink. We don't want them fully cooked yet.

Push the ingredients to the side of the wok and add the rice noodles, followed by the soy sauces and the oyster sauce. Stir-fry until some of the noodles get a little charred – this will take less than 1 minute.

Push the ingredients to the side of the wok again and crack in the eggs. Let them cook undisturbed for about 20 seconds, then break the yolks and quickly mix everything together. Add the bean sprouts and garlic chives and stir-fry for 30–40 seconds.

Serve immediately, straight from the wok.

NOTE: If you are using a small chopper or blender, add all the ingredients except the lime juice and blend to a smooth paste. Then stir in the lime juice.

The chilli paste will keep in an airtight container in the fridge for up to 2 weeks.

If any dish has a cult-following, it's ramen. A perfectly crafted bowl of broth is the base for this Japanese icon, but what flavour you choose is up to you. This recipe uses miso and is vegan, from the broth to the toppings.

SERVES 2

2 tbsp white miso paste

2 tbsp mirin

1 tbsp sake

1 tsp caster (superfine) sugar

1½ tbsp peanut oil

2 tsp toasted sesame oil

150 g (5½ oz) Japanese eggplant (aubergine), cut into 3 cm (1¼ in) cubes

120 g (4½ oz) carrot, julienned

240 g (8½ oz) fresh ramen noodles

2 portions Vegan broth (see page 137), simmering

200 g (7 oz) smoked tofu, cut into 6 slices

50 g (1¾ oz) bean sprouts

2 tsp toasted sesame seeds

chilli oil, for drizzling

UMAMI MUSHROOM POWDER

20 g (¾ oz) dried shiitake mushrooms

40 g (⅓ cup) sea salt flakes

1 tbsp gochugaru (Korean chilli powder)

½ tsp black peppercorns

To make the umami mushroom powder, place all the ingredients in a spice grinder and pulverise to a powder. Set aside (see Note).

In a small bowl, whisk together the miso paste, mirin, sake and sugar.

Bring a saucepan of water to a rolling boil over high heat. Meanwhile, heat the oils in a wok over medium–high heat. Add the eggplant and stir-fry for about 4–5 minutes, then add the carrot and stir-fry for a further 1 minute. Add the miso mixture and stir-fry for another minute.

In the saucepan of boiling water, cook the noodles according to the packet instructions. Drain and divide between two serving bowls.

Pour over the hot vegan broth. Add the vegetables, smoked tofu, bean sprouts and sesame seeds.

Drizzle over the chilli oil and garnish with the umami mushroom powder.

NOTE: Sprinkle over ramen, eggs, veggies, or anything else you're inspired to for a spiced umami hit. The powder will keep in a sealed jar in the pantry for up to 6 months.

PANKO CHICKEN SHIO RAMEN

Up next in the foundational ramen flavours is *shio*, or salt. Featuring a lighter broth than miso or *shoyu* ramens (pages 49 and 52), this recipe is topped with fried chicken for a bowl of true comfort food.

SERVES 2

2 × 150 g (5½ oz) chicken breasts, pounded until 1 cm (½ in) thick

sea salt and freshly ground black pepper

50 g (⅓ cup) plain (all-purpose) flour

1 egg, beaten

60 g (1 cup) panko breadcrumbs

peanut oil, for shallow-frying

240 g (8½ oz) fresh ramen noodles

2 portions Shio broth (see page 138), simmering

8 slices menma (fermented bamboo shoots)

100 g (3½ oz) English spinach, blanched and squeezed dry

2 spring (green) onions, finely sliced

tonkatsu sauce, for drizzling (optional) (see Note)

2 Onsen tamago (see page 130), to serve

Season the chicken with salt and pepper. Place the flour in a shallow bowl, the beaten egg in a second bowl and the breadcrumbs in a third. Dredge the chicken in the flour and shake off the excess. Dip into the egg, then coat in the breadcrumbs.

Bring a saucepan of water to a rolling boil over high heat. Meanwhile, heat 3 cm (1¼ in) of oil in a wok to 190°C (375°F). Fry the chicken for 2–3 minutes on each side until golden brown and cooked through.

In the saucepan of boiling water, cook the noodles according to the packet instructions. Drain and divide between two serving bowls.

Pour over the hot shio broth. Slice the chicken into 5–6 slices each and lay on top of the noodles. Add the bamboo shoots, spinach and spring onion. Finish with a drizzle of tonkatsu sauce over the chicken, if using, and serve with the onsen tamago on the side.

NOTE: Tonkatsu sauce can be purchased from most Asian supermarkets.

Another traditional ramen flavour is *shoyu*, or soy sauce. To finish this recipe off, pork *karaage* is added on top. Coated in aromatics, sake, soy sauce and then fried, these bites of pork are reason enough to make this dish.

SERVES 2

2 tsp dried wakame

240 g (8½ oz) fresh ramen noodles

2 portions Shoyu broth (see page 139), simmering

2 slices narutomaki fish cake

20 g (¾ oz) enoki mushrooms

1 Ajitsuke tamago (see page 130), halved

2 spring (green) onions, finely sliced

Japanese quick pickles (see page 132), to serve

PORK KARAAGE

2 garlic cloves, finely grated

10 g (¼ oz) ginger, finely grated

1 tbsp soy sauce

1½ tbsp sake

2 tsp toasted sesame oil

300 g (10½ oz) pork loin, cut into 4 cm (1½ in) pieces

peanut oil, for deep-frying

80 g (2¾ oz) potato starch

¼ tsp sea salt

¼ tsp ground white pepper

Rinse the wakame and rehydrate in a bowl of cold water. Drain well.

To make the pork karaage, combine the garlic, ginger, soy sauce, sake and sesame oil in a bowl. Add the pork, stir to coat, then cover and refrigerate for 30 minutes.

Heat enough oil for deep-frying in a deep-fryer or wok to 190°C (375°F).

Combine the potato starch, salt and pepper in a bowl.

Remove the pork from the fridge, drain and discard the marinade.

Toss the pork through the potato starch, coating thoroughly. Fry the pork in batches for 3–4 minutes until cooked through. Drain on a wire rack.

Bring a saucepan of water to a rolling boil over high heat. Cook the noodles according to the packet instructions and drain. Divide the noodles between two serving bowls.

Pour over the hot shoyu broth. Add the wakame, narutomaki, enoki mushrooms, ajitsuke tamago and spring onion. Top with the pork karaage and serve with Japanese pickles on the side.

Tonkotsu ramen is a great dish when you have a whole afternoon free: the product of hours of boiling pork bones, this creamy broth is a testament that good things take time. *Chashu*, a Japanese braised pork, completes the dish, with bamboo shoots and a seasoned egg.

SERVES 2

6 slices Chashu pork (see page 128)

2 tsp Rendered pork fat (see page 129)

2 portions (120 g/4½ oz each) thin ramen noodles

2 portions Tonkotsu broth (see page 140), simmering

20 g (¾ oz) fresh wood ear mushrooms, sliced

8 slices menma (fermented bamboo shoots)

1 tbsp Wakame gomasio

2 Ajitsuke tamago (see page 130), halved

1 nori sheet, cut into quarters

Black mayu (see page 135), for drizzling

2 tsp finely sliced garlic chives

WAKAME GOMASIO

155 g (1 cup) sesame seeds

1 piece (6–7 g/¼ oz) dried wakame

2 tbsp sea salt flakes

To make the wakame gomasio, preheat the oven to 160°C (320°F). Toast the sesame seeds in a heavy-based frying pan over very low heat for 5–6 minutes until they take on a deep golden brown colour and a buttery aroma. Remove from the pan and set aside to cool completely.

Place the wakame on a baking tray and toast in the oven for 9–10 minutes. Set aside to cool completely.

Transfer the sesame seeds, wakame and the salt to a food processor and pulse for about 30 seconds, until the ingredients are quite finely ground but still with a few whole seeds. Set aside (see Note).

Cook the chashu slices and pork fat in a large frying pan over medium heat until warm and melting. Meanwhile, bring a saucepan of water to a rolling boil over high heat. Cook the noodles according to the packet instructions and drain. Divide the noodles between two serving bowls.

Pour over the hot tonkotsu broth. Top with the wood ear mushrooms, bamboo shoots, wakame gomasio, ajitsuke tamago, nori pieces and chashu slices. Drizzle over the remaining pork fat from the frying pan and a little black mayu. Finish with a sprinkle of garlic chives.

NOTE: Sprinkle *Wakame gomasio* over your favourite ramen toppings or blend into your broth of choice. Store in a sealed jar in the pantry for up to 3 weeks.

T A N T A N M E N

A Chinese dish from Japan and a close relative of Dan dan noodles (page 14). Unlike its cousin, *Tantanmen* is served with a broth, and the flavours are not identical. They do share, however, delicious, savoury minced meat and the temptation to keep eating even after you're full.

SERVES 2

1 baby bok choy (pak choy), quartered lengthwise

90 g (1 cup) bean sprouts

320 g (11½ oz) fresh ramen noodles

1 soft-boiled egg, halved (see page 61)

1 spring (green) onion, green part only, finely sliced

1 tsp toasted white sesame seeds

red chilli oil, to taste

shichimi togarashi, to taste (optional)

RAMEN BROTH

3 tbsp Mentsuyu (see page 136)

2 tbsp Chinese sesame paste

1 tbsp Sichuan crispy chilli oil (see page 133)

250 ml (1 cup) water

500 ml (2 cups) unsweetened soy milk

2 tsp chicken bouillon

SPICY PORK TOPPING

1 tbsp vegetable oil

3 garlic cloves, grated

1 tsp grated ginger

1 tbsp spicy doubanjiang

1 tbsp light soy sauce

250 g (9 oz) minced (ground) pork

2 tbsp sake

First make the ramen broth. Put the mentsuyu, sesame paste and chilli oil in a bowl and mix well. Divide the mixture between serving bowls and set aside. Pour the water and soy milk into a saucepan, add the chicken bouillon and bring to a simmer over medium heat. Reduce the heat until the broth is barely bubbling, cover with a lid and keep warm.

Next make the spicy pork topping. Heat the oil in a wok over medium–high heat. Add the garlic and ginger, and stir-fry until fragrant, about 10 seconds. Add the doubanjiang and soy sauce, and stir-fry for another 10 seconds. Add the minced pork, breaking it up as you stir-fry for 3 minutes. Add the cooking sake and cook until most of the sauce has evaporated, about 30 seconds. Turn off the heat and cover to keep warm.

Bring a large saucepan of water to a rolling boil over high heat. Blanch the bok choy for 1 minute, remove using a wire skimmer and set aside. Blanch the bean sprouts for 30 seconds, remove, shake off excess water and set aside with the bok choy.

In the same saucepan of boiling water, cook the noodles according to the packet instructions.

Meanwhile, pour the hot broth into each serving bowl on top of the chilli mixture. Drain the noodles, shake off excess water and divide equally between bowls. Top with the boy choy, bean sprouts, spicy pork topping and half an egg. Scatter over the spring onion and sesame seeds, add a few drops of chilli oil and a smidgen of shichimi togarashi to taste, if using, and serve.

CRISPY EBI RAMEN

Who says you can't have crispy, fried food and noodle soup at the same time? This delicious combination of crispy *ebi* (prawn) and noodles brings together two of the world's great culinary creations.

SERVES 1

180 g (6½ oz) fresh ramen noodles

2 slices narutomaki fish cake

1 spring (green) onion, finely sliced

shichimi togarashi, to taste

RAMEN BROTH

125 ml (½ cup) Mentsuyu sauce (see page 136)

500 ml (2 cups) Dashi (see page 136)

CRISPY EBI

2-4 fresh large prawns (shrimp), peeled and deveined, tails intact

75 g (½ cup) self-raising flour

125 ml (½ cup) iced water

30 g (½ cup) panko crumbs

vegetable oil, for frying

Prepare the ramen broth by placing both ingredients in a medium saucepan, then bring to a simmer over low heat. Reduce the heat until the broth is barely bubbling, cover with a lid and keep warm.

To make the crispy ebi, wash the prawns, pat them dry and lay them flat. Sift the flour and a pinch of salt into a bowl. Whisk the iced water in until the mixture is lightly lumpy – don't over mix. Place 2 tablespoons of flour and the panko crumbs in two separate bowls.

Pour enough oil to submerge the prawns into a saucepan and heat to 180°C (350°F) over medium heat. The oil is ready when a wooden chopstick lowered into the oil fizzes. Dredge each prawn cutlet in flour, shake off excess, dip it in the batter and then coat it evenly in panko crumbs. Drop it into the hot oil and cook until a light golden colour, about 2 minutes. Transfer prawns to a wire rack, season with salt and keep warm.

Bring a saucepan of water to a rolling boil over high heat. Tease apart the ramen noodles as you drop them into the water. Stir and cook according to the packet instructions, no more than 2 minutes. Drain and shake off excess water.

Place the noodles into a serving bowl. Pour the ramen broth over the noodles. Place the prawns and fish cake slices on top, garnish with spring onion, sprinkle with shichimi togarashi as desired and serve.

Kake udon (Udon noodle soup) is made with a dashi broth that's poured over the chewy noodles. Spring onion is the traditional topping, and others can be added or left off depending how simple you want to keep things. In other words, if you just really want noodles, this is a soup for you.

SERVES 2

600 ml (20½ fl oz) Dashi (see page 136)

2 tbsp light soy sauce

1 tbsp mirin

1 tsp granulated sugar

pinch of salt

400 g (14 oz) parboiled udon noodles

TOPPINGS

4 slices narutomaki fish cake

2 tbsp tinned sweetcorn kernels

1 soft-boiled egg, halved

2 spring (green) onions, green parts only, finely sliced

To make the soft-boiled egg, bring a small saucepan of water to a simmer over medium heat. Gently drop the egg in and cook for 6 minutes. Remove the egg and place in a bowl of iced water. Peel the egg and cut in half when ready to serve.

Place the dashi, soy sauce, mirin, sugar and salt in a medium saucepan. Bring the broth to a simmer over medium heat. Once simmering, turn off the heat, cover with a lid and set aside.

Bring a saucepan of water to a rolling boil over high heat. Cook the noodles according to the packet instructions. Drain and rinse the noodles under running water until the noodles are cool enough to touch. Shake off excess water, then divide the noodles between serving bowls. Pour the hot broth over the noodles, and top each bowl with fish cake slices, corn kernels, half an egg and spring onion to serve.

KITSUNE UDON

A soup for humans and foxes. This dish features a favourite treat of *kitsune*, the fox guardians in Japanese folklore – fried tofu pouches. While we don't encourage you to leave out a bowl for wildlife, this soup is rich with dashi and is a staple of Japanese noodles.

SERVES 2

400 g (14 oz) parboiled udon noodles

4 pieces inari age (fried tofu pouches)

6 slices narutomaki fish cake

1 spring (green) onion, finely sliced

shichimi togarashi, to taste (optional)

BROTH

500 ml (2 cups) Dashi (see page 136)

1 tbsp mirin

1 tsp granulated sugar

1 tbsp light soy sauce

salt, to taste

To make the broth, place all the ingredients into a saucepan and bring to the boil over medium heat. Once boiling, turn off the heat, cover with a lid and keep warm.

Bring a large saucepan of water to a rolling boil over high heat. Cook the noodles according to the packet instructions. Drain and rinse the noodles under running water until the noodles are cool enough to touch. Shake off excess water.

Divide the noodles between serving bowls. Pour the hot broth over the noodles. Top with the inari age, fish cake slices and spring onion. Sprinkle with a smidgen of the shichimi togarashi, if using, and serve.

KARE UDON

Tokyo gave us Curry udon, combining thick udon noodles with a rich curry soup. Japanese curry is known for being milder and sweeter than curries from other countries, and *Kare udon* is no exception. Here, it is mixed with dashi and mirin to create a fragrant bowl of soup.

SERVES 2

1 tbsp vegetable oil

½ large onion, finely sliced

180 g (6¼ oz) pork loin, thinly sliced (about 3 mm/⅛ in thick)

1 tbsp mirin

750 ml (3 cups) Dashi (see page 136)

2 cubes Japanese curry roux (see Note)

400 g (14 oz) parboiled udon noodles

1 spring (green) onion, green part only, finely sliced

Heat the oil in a medium saucepan over medium–high heat. Add the onion and sauté until translucent, about 1 minute. Add the pork and cook for 3 minutes. Add the mirin and dashi, cover with a lid, reduce the heat to low and cook for 5 minutes.

Put the curry roux cubes in a heatproof bowl and pour two ladlefuls of the hot broth on the cubes. Use chopsticks or a fork and stir until the cubes are fully dissolved. Pour the mixture into the saucepan and stir to mix well. Reduce the heat to low and let it simmer while preparing the noodles.

Bring a saucepan of water to a rolling boil over high heat. Cook the noodles according to the packet instructions. Drain and rinse the noodles under running water until the noodles are cool enough to touch.

Shake off excess water and divide the noodles between serving bowls, then spoon ladlefuls of the curry soup over the top. Garnish with spring onion and serve.

NOTE: Japanese curry roux comes in a cube form that can be found at many Asian supermarkets. They come in many different flavours and levels of heat, so choose one that best suits your palate.

This beef noodle soup is packed with spices and topped with beef that's cooked until it's extra tender. An iconic dish, loaded with fresh noodles, bok choy and pickled mustard greens, it's worth the time.

SERVES 4–6

2 tbsp vegetable oil, plus extra

1 kg (2 lb 3 oz) gravy or chuck beef, cubed

1 large onion, quartered

5 cm (2 in) piece ginger, smashed

8 garlic cloves, smashed

3 spring (green) onions, cut into 5 om (2 in) lengths

2 large tomatoes, chopped

5 dried red chillies, chopped

600 g (1 lb 5 oz) fresh Chinese wheat (white) noodles

2 bunches baby bok choy (pak choy), separated

200 g (7 oz) pickled mustard greens

a handful coriander (cilantro) leaves, to serve

a handful Roasted peanuts (see page 133), to serve

BRAISING LIQUID

500 ml (2 cups) chicken stock

125 ml (½ cup) Shaoxing rice wine

125 ml (½ cup) light soy sauce

3 tbsp dark soy sauce

3 tbsp dark brown sugar

2 tbsp spicy doubanjiang

SPICES

1 cinnamon stick

2 star anise

2 tsp fennel seeds

2 tsp Sichuan peppercorns

2 tsp black peppercorns

Place all the ingredients for the braising liquid in a large bowl and stir until the sugar has dissolved.

Heat the oil in a large saucepan or Dutch oven over medium–high heat. Working in batches, sear the beef in a single layer, turning occasionally, until browned on all sides, about 5 minutes. Transfer the beef to a large plate and set aside. Top up the oil as necessary before searing each batch of beef.

To the same saucepan, add the onion, ginger, garlic, spring onions, tomatoes and dried chillies, and stirring frequently, cook until the onions are translucent and the tomatoes are breaking down, about 5 minutes.

Give the braising liquid a quick stir and add to the saucepan. Stir, scraping the bottom of the saucepan to dislodge any caramelised bits. Return the beef and all its juice to the saucepan, add all the spices and pour in about 2 litres (2 quarts) of water until the beef is close to fully submerged. Bring to the boil, then reduce the heat to low, cover with a lid that is slightly ajar and simmer until the beef is tender, about 3 hours.

Once ready, carefully transfer the beef to a heatproof bowl using tongs and a strainer. Strain the braising liquid through a fine-mesh sieve into a fresh saucepan. Discard the remaining solids. Return the beef to the braising liquid. Keep warm over a very low heat while preparing the noodles.

Bring a saucepan of water to a rolling boil over high heat. Place one portion of the noodles (around 150 g/5½ oz) and 2–3 bok choy leaves into a mesh strainer, lower it into the hot water and cook for 1 minute, stirring occasionally with chopsticks. Lift the strainer out, drain, reserving the water, and shake off excess water. Transfer the noodles to an individual serving bowl and pour 125 ml (½ cup) of the reserved water over the noodles. Repeat for each portion of the noodles.

Top each bowl with a few chunks of the beef, then ladle the broth over the top. Add a generous mound of pickled mustard greens, coriander and peanuts, and serve.

JANCHI GUKSU

In Korea, *Janchi guksu* (Festive noodle soup) is traditionally prepared for special occasions, but don't let that stop you from cooking it every day. Full of long noodles, which symbolise good health and longevity in Korea, there's more reasons than just the flavour to cook up a large bowl.

SERVES 4

1 zucchini (courgette)

1 tsp salt, plus extra for sautéing

60 ml (¼ cup) vegetable oil

1 bunch English spinach, rinsed and cut into 5 cm (2 in) lengths

2 eggs, beaten

Dashima myeolchi yuksu (Anchovy and kelp stock) (see page 141)

450 g (1 lb) thin wheat flour noodles (somyeon)

1 tsp toasted sesame seeds

Yangnyeomjang (Spicy soy and spring onion sauce), to serve

YANGNYEOMJANG

60 ml (¼ cup) soy sauce

2 tbsp rice (or white) vinegar

6 garlic cloves, crushed

2 tsp caster (superfine) sugar

2 tbsp gochugaru (Korean chilli flakes)

½ tsp freshly ground black pepper

2–3 spring (green) onions, finely sliced

To make the yangnyeomjang, combine all the ingredients in a small bowl and stir until the sugar has dissolved. Set aside (see Note).

Cut the zucchini in half lengthways, then cut each half on an angle into thin 3 mm (⅛ in) slices. Combine the sliced zucchini and salt in a bowl, mix well, and set aside for 10 minutes. Then use your hands to squeeze out as much liquid as possible from the zucchini.

Heat 1 tablespoon of the vegetable oil in a frying pan over medium heat and sauté the zucchini for 1–2 minutes, until softened. Transfer to a plate.

Heat another tablespoon of the oil in the same frying pan and cook the spinach for 1 minute, or until softened. Season to taste with salt and stir-fry for another minute, then transfer to the plate with the zucchini.

Heat the remaining oil in the same frying pan, add the beaten egg, then swirl the pan around to spread the egg into a thin layer. Fry for 2 minutes, then flip the omelette over and fry for another minute or until lightly golden. Transfer the omelette to a chopping board and cut into thin strips. Transfer to the plate with the spinach and zucchini.

Bring the anchovy and kelp stock to a simmer over low heat, ready for serving.

Prepare a large bowl of iced water and set aside.

Bring a large saucepan of water to the boil over high heat and cook the wheat flour noodles according to the packet instructions. Drain, then immediately refresh in the iced water to stop the cooking process. Leave to chill for 2–3 minutes. Briefly stir the noodles around in the water to loosen them up, then drain.

Divide the noodles among four serving bowls. Pour ladles of hot stock into each bowl, then top the noodles with the zucchini, spinach and egg. Garnish with sesame seeds and serve with spicy soy and spring onion sauce on the side.

NOTE: *Yangnyeomjang* will keep in an airtight container in the fridge for up to 5 days.

P H O B O

Originating in the late 1800s, *Phở bò* is perhaps Vietnam's most famous dish. The fat from the beef and the fragrance of the spices make these noodles truly delicious.

SERVES 8–10

2 kg (4 lb 6 oz) fresh pho noodles (see page 74)

1 kg (2 lb 3 oz) beef blade steak, very thinly sliced

1 onion, finely sliced

1 bunch spring (green) onions, finely sliced

1 bunch coriander (cilantro), leaves picked

BROTH

5 kg (11 lb) beef marrowbones

200 g (7 oz) piece ginger, unpeeled

2 large onions, unpeeled

1 garlic bulb, unpeeled, halved

500 g (1 lb 2 oz) beef brisket

1 kg (2 lb 3 oz) oxtail

15 star anise

2 black cardamom pods

2 cassia bark sticks

4 cloves

1 tbsp coriander seeds

60 g (2 oz) sea salt

200 ml (7 fl oz) fish sauce

50 g (1¾ oz) caster (superfine) sugar

ACCOMPANIMENTS

1 kg (2 lb 3 oz) bean sprouts

2 bunches Thai basil

lemon wedges

6 bird's eye chillies, sliced

hoi sin sauce

sriracha chilli sauce

fish sauce

To make the broth, rinse the marrowbones to remove any blood and splinters, then transfer to a 10 litre (2½ gallon) stockpot. Fill the pot with enough cold water to cover the bones, then place over high heat and bring to the boil. Boil the bones for 20–30 minutes, until no more blood comes to the surface. Drain and discard the cooking liquid, and rinse any remaining blood or impurities from the bones. Return the bones to a clean stockpot, cover with water to nearly the top of the pot and bring back to the boil.

Meanwhile, roast the ginger, onion and garlic under a hot grill (broiler) until the skins are charred. Add to the stockpot, along with the brisket and oxtail. Simmer for about 3 hours, removing any impurities as they rise to the surface, or until the meat is tender. Remove the brisket from the broth and set aside to cool, then place in the fridge to use later in the soup. Leave the oxtail in the broth.

Bring the stock back to the boil and continue to remove any impurities that rise to the surface. Simmer gently over medium heat for 7–8 hours until the broth has reduced by 20–30 per cent.

After 5–6 hours of cooking, lightly toast the whole spices in a dry frying pan over medium heat until fragrant. Tie the spices in a square of muslin (cheesecloth) and add to the stockpot for the last few hours of cooking.

When the broth is ready, remove and discard the solids. Strain the broth through a fine-mesh sieve into a clean saucepan. Season the broth with the salt and fish sauce, and add the sugar if you feel the broth needs a little sweetness. Return to a low heat and simmer until ready to serve.

Bring a large saucepan of water to the boil. Using a noodle basket (see Note on page 74), blanch individual portions of pho noodles (about 120 g–150 g/4 oz–5½ oz per person) for 10 seconds, then transfer to large serving bowls.

Slice the brisket into 2 mm (⅛ in) thick slices and evenly divide among bowls. Top with the thinly sliced beef blade, onion, spring onion and coriander. Ladle the stock into the bowls, ensuring that it's boiling hot to cook the raw beef.

Place the accompaniments on a serving platter, serve the pho and invite guests to season and flavour their own dish.

If you've never made pho before, *Phở gà* is a great place to start. Its broth is light, but it's still packed with the flavours that have made pho synonymous with Vietnamese cuisine around the world.

SERVES 8–10

2 kg (4 lb 6 oz) fresh pho noodles (see page 74)

1 onion, finely sliced

1 bunch spring (green) onions, finely sliced

1 bunch coriander (cilantro), leaves picked

BROTH

3 kg (6 lb 10 oz) chicken bones

200 g (7 oz) piece ginger, unpeeled

2 large onions, unpeeled

1 garlic bulb, unpeeled, halved

1 × 1 kg (2 lb 3 oz) free-range chicken

6 star anise

2 black cardamom pods

1 small cassia bark stick

50 g (1¾ oz) coriander seeds

3 tbsp sea salt

200 ml (7 fl oz) fish sauce

50 g (1¾ oz) caster (superfine) sugar

ACCOMPANIMENTS

1 kg (2 lb 3 oz) bean sprouts

2 bunches Thai basil

6 bird's eye chillies, sliced

lemon wedges

sriracha chilli sauce

hoisin sauce

Lemongrass sate (see page 135)

fish sauce

To make the broth, rinse the chicken bones to remove any blood and splinters, then transfer to a 10 litre (2½ gallon) stockpot. Fill the pot with enough cold water to cover the bones, then place over high heat and bring to the boil. Boil the bones for 20–30 minutes, until no more blood comes to the surface. Drain and discard the cooking liquid, and rinse any remaining blood or impurities from the bones. Return the bones to a clean stockpot, cover with water to nearly the top of the pot and bring back to the boil.

Meanwhile, roast the ginger, onion and garlic over a gas stovetop or barbecue flame, or under the grill (broiler) until the skins are blistered and aromatic. Rinse off any burnt bits and add, whole, to the broth, along with the whole chicken. Poach the chicken for 15–20 minutes until cooked through, then remove from the broth and set aside to cool.

Remove the chicken meat from the bones and return the bones to the broth. Tear the chicken meat into smaller pieces and set aside.

Toast the star anise, cardamom pods, cassia bark and coriander seeds in a dry frying pan over medium heat until fragrant. Tie the spices in a square of muslin (cheesecloth) and drop it into the broth. Continue to gently simmer the broth over medium heat for a further 4–5 hours until the broth has reduced by 20–30 per cent.

When the stock is ready, remove and discard the bones, old hen and spices. Strain the stock through a fine-mesh sieve into a clean saucepan. Season the stock with the salt, fish sauce and sugar. Return to a low heat and simmer until ready to serve.

Bring a large saucepan of water to the boil. Blanch individual portions (see Note on page 74) of the pho noodles (about 120 g–150 g/4 oz–5½ oz per person) for 10 seconds, then transfer to large serving bowls. Evenly divide the chicken among the bowls, pour over the hot stock and top with the onion, spring onion and coriander.

Place the accompaniments on a serving platter, serve the pho and invite guests to season and flavour their own dish

PHO CHAY

While Beef pho and Chicken pho (pages 70 and 73) are off vegans' menus, there's no reason they can't enjoy *Phở chay*. Instead of bones, this broth's rounded flavour is created with vegetables.

SERVES 6–8

1 kg (2 lb 3 oz) fresh pho noodles (see Note)

500 g (1 lb 2 oz) organic tofu, cubed

200 g (7 oz) enoki mushrooms, separated

200 g (7 oz) oyster mushrooms

1 red onion, finely sliced

1 bunch spring (green) onions, finely sliced

1 bunch coriander leaves (cilantro), leaves picked

BROTH

2 carrots

1 small wombok (Chinese cabbage)

½ white cabbage

250 g (9 oz) ginger, unpeeled

1 onion, unpeeled

1 garlic bulb, unpeeled, halved

4 star anise

1 black cardamom pod

1 small cassia bark stick

50 g (1¾ oz) coriander seeds

3 tbsp salt, to taste

1 tbsp caster (superfine) sugar, to taste

ACCOMPANIMENTS

500 g (1 lb 2 oz) bean sprouts

1 bunch Thai basil

5 bird's eye chillies, sliced

lemon wedges

hoisin sauce

To make the broth, place the carrots, wombok and cabbage in a 10 litre (2½ gallon) stockpot and cover with water to nearly the top of the pot. Place over high heat, bring to the boil and skim off any scum that rises to the surface. Reduce to a simmer.

Meanwhile, roast the ginger, onion and garlic over a gas stovetop or barbecue flame, or under the grill (broiler) until the skins are blistered and aromatic. Rinse off any burnt bits and add, whole, to the broth.

Toast the star anise, cardamom pod, cassia bark and coriander seeds in a dry frying pan over medium heat until fragrant. Tie the spices in a square of muslin (cheesecloth) and drop it into the broth. Continue to simmer the broth over medium heat for 3–4 hours until it has reduced by 20–30 per cent. Strain the broth into a clean saucepan and season with the salt and sugar. Return the broth to a simmer. Discard the solids.

Bring a large saucepan of water to the boil. Blanch individual portions (see Note) of the pho noodles (about 120 g–150 g/4 oz–5½ oz per person) for 10 seconds, then transfer to large serving bowls. Evenly divide the tofu and mushrooms among the bowls, pour over the hot broth and top with the onion, spring onion and coriander.

Place the accompaniments on a serving platter, serve the pho and invite guests to season and flavour their own dish

NOTE: Fresh pho noodles can be purchased from most Asian supermarkets. If you are unable to find them, you can also use dried thin rice stick noodles (sometimes referred to as pad thai noodles). Cook according to the packet instructions, then drain and divide among serving bowls.

It's best to use an Asian noodle-blanching basket to cook the noodles. These can be purchased from Asian kitchen supply stores or online.

LAU

When you're sharing a meal, Hotpot is the perfect choice. Cooked at the table, *Lẩu* is as much an activity as a dish. Pick your meat and veg of choice and add them to the pot with – of course – noodles.

SERVES 4–6

Hotpot dipping sauce (page 134)

2 litres (2 quarts) Chicken broth

2 tsp sea salt

2 tsp caster (superfine) sugar

small handful coriander (cilantro) leaves

3 spring (green) onions, finely sliced

500 g (1 lb 2 oz) dried instant egg noodles

CHICKEN BROTH

1 kg (2 lb 3 oz) chicken bones

1 × 1 kg (2 lb 3 oz) free-range chicken

1 onion, peeled

2 garlic cloves

VEGETABLES

200 g (7 oz) shimeji mushrooms

200 g (7 oz) oyster mushrooms

200 g (7 oz) water spinach

2 bunches bok choy (pak choy), quartered

MEAT AND SEAFOOD

200 g (7 oz) squid, cleaned and hoods scored (optional)

12 fresh prawns (shrimp), peeled and deveined

4 cooked blue swimmer crabs (optional)

300 g (10½ oz) sirloin beef, very thinly sliced

12 fish balls (see Note)

12 beef balls (see Note)

6 fish cakes (see Note)

For this recipe, you will need a portable gas stove that can sit in the centre of your table. You can buy these at Asian kitchenware stores or camping stores.

To make the broth, rinse the chicken bones to remove any blood and splinters. Transfer to a large stockpot, add the chicken and cover with 3 litres (3 quarts) water. Bring to the boil, skimming off any impurities that rise to the top, then reduce the heat to a simmer, add the onion and garlic and cook for 30 minutes. Remove the chicken from the broth and set aside to cool. Strain the broth and discard the solids.

Divide the dipping sauce among individual ramekins for dipping.

Place the stove on the table. Pour the chicken broth into a large hotpot and place the hotpot on the stove over medium heat. Season with the salt and sugar and add the coriander and spring onion.

Place the raw ingredients in bowls or on plates, keeping the meat and seafood separate, and distribute around the table.

Wait until the broth comes to the boil, then invite guests to select and cook their own ingredients.

The following are approximate cooking times for each ingredient, depending on their size:

Dried instant egg noodles: 5–8 minutes

Mushrooms: 5–7 minutes

Water spinach and bok choy: 3–7 minutes

Squid: 4–5 minutes

Prawns: 3–5 minutes

Blue swimmer crabs: just heat through

Sirloin beef: 1 minute

Fish balls, beef balls and fish cakes: just heat through

NOTE: Fish balls, beef balls and fish cakes can be purchased from Asian supermarkets.

This Coconut curry soup comes from Northern Thailand. *Khao soi* is creamy and rich, full of aromatics that make it worth eating ladle after ladle. Made with coconut milk and chicken, it's a good dish for when you're craving a depth of flavour.

SERVES 4

1 cup vegetable oil, for frying

600 g (1 lb 5 oz) fresh flat egg wonton noodles (see Note)

1 × 400 ml (14 fl oz) tin coconut milk

3 tbsp fish sauce

250 ml (1 cup) chicken stock

2 tbsp palm sugar (or dark brown sugar)

300 g (10½ oz) boneless, skinless chicken thighs, cut into strips

lime wedges, to serve

pickled mustard greens, to serve

a handful coriander (cilantro) leaves, to serve

fried shallots, to serve

CURRY PASTE

10 g (¼ oz) dried red chillies, soaked in hot water for 20 minutes and drained

2 medium shallots

5 garlic cloves, peeled

2.5 cm (1 in) piece ginger, peeled

2.5 cm (1 in) piece turmeric, peeled

7 g (¼ cup) coriander (cilantro) leaves

zest and juice of 1 lime

1 tbsp shrimp paste (kapi) (see Note)

Heat the oil in a small saucepan over medium–high heat. Place a handful of the noodles in the hot oil and fry until golden brown and crunchy, about 20 seconds. Remove the fried noodles using a strainer and set aside.

To make the curry paste, put all the ingredients in a food processor and blend into a fine paste. If it is too dry to blend, add a tablespoon of water to the mixture.

Heat 2 tablespoons of the frying oil in a large saucepan over medium–high heat. Add the curry paste and stir-fry until fragrant, about 5 minutes. Add the coconut milk and stir to dislodge any caramelised bits stuck to the bottom. Add the fish sauce, chicken stock and palm sugar and bring to the boil. Add the chicken to the soup, stir and bring to the boil again. Reduce the heat to medium–low and simmer while preparing the noodles.

Bring a saucepan of water to a rolling boil over high heat. Place one portion of the noodles (around 150 g/5½ oz) into a mesh strainer, lower it into the hot water and cook for 1 minute, stirring the noodles occasionally with chopsticks. Lift the strainer out, drain and shake off excess water, then transfer the noodles to an individual serving bowl. Repeat for each portion of the noodles.

Spoon ladlefuls of the curry broth and chicken pieces over the noodles. Top with a lime wedge, the pickled mustard greens, coriander and fried shallots, and a generous mound of the fried noodles and serve.

NOTE: Fresh flat egg wonton noodles can be found at Asian supermarkets.

Kapi is a Thai paste made from fermenting krill (tiny shrimp-like crustaceans). They're then dried and ground into a paste that can be found at Asian supermarkets.

ASAM LAKSA

Laksa is one of the most popular dishes in Malaysia, with plenty of regional variations. This version has an aromatic, tangy broth made with fresh mackerel and tamarind. Top it off with a spoonful of shrimp paste for an authentic flavour and eat it any time of the day.

SERVES 4

80 ml (⅓ cup) vegetable oil

2 tbsp granulated sugar, plus extra if needed

80 g (⅓ cup) tamarind paste

1 bunch Vietnamese mint

2 tsp salt, or to taste

2 tbsp fish sauce, or to taste

250 g (9 oz) dried laksa noodles

hae kor (shrimp paste) (see Note), to serve

LAKSA BROTH

1 kg (2 lb 3 oz) whole mackerel, cleaned

6 slices dried tamarind

LAKSA PASTE

20 dried chillies, seeded

2 red onions, roughly chopped

1 tbsp toasted belacan (shrimp paste)

1 lemongrass stalk, white part only

CONDIMENTS

1 long cucumber, julienned

1 red onion, finely sliced

1 iceberg lettuce, finely sliced

4 bird's eye chillies, halved and sliced

1 small pineapple, peeled, cored and diced

1 bunch mint

To make the laksa broth, bring 2 litres (2 quarts) of water to the boil in a large saucepan. Add the fish and dried tamarind and boil for 10 minutes. Transfer the cooked fish to a bowl and strain the stock.

With clean hands, pick the flesh off the fish and discard the bones. Break the fish meat into bite-sized pieces, then return it to the stock and set aside.

To make the laksa paste, place all the ingredients in a food processor and process to a fine paste.

Heat the oil in a wok over medium heat, add the laksa paste and sauté for 5–7 minutes, until it smells aromatic and the oil has separated. Add the sugar and stir for another minute. Pour in the laksa stock and add the tamarind paste and Vietnamese mint. Cover and bring to the boil over medium heat. Check the broth and season to taste with salt, fish sauce and sugar.

Prepare the noodles according to the packet instructions.

To serve, divide the noodles among bowls, pour over the laksa broth and top with the condiments. Serve immediately with a spoonful of hae kor.

NOTE: *Hae kor* is a salty-sweet and fragrant condiment, frequently added in Malaysia to salads or used as a topping on *Asam laksa*.

COLD SESAME NOODLES

Cold sesame noodles aren't firmly tied to a specific cuisine, which means one thing: this combination was meant to be. The dressing, made with sesame paste, peanut butter and chilli oil, is a match made for noodles.

SERVES 4

450 g (1 lb) pre-steamed hokkien noodles (see Note)

20 g (¾ oz) Roasted peanuts (see page 133), plus extra

2 spring (green) onions, finely sliced

½ short cucumber, peeled, deseeded and julienned into 5 cm (2 in) lengths

1 tbsp toasted sesame seeds

Sichuan crispy chilli oil, to taste (optional) (see page 133)

PEANUT SESAME DRESSING

2 tbsp Chinese sesame paste (see Note)

2 tbsp smooth peanut butter

1 tbsp light soy sauce

½ tbsp granulated sugar

½ tbsp black vinegar

1 tbsp sesame oil

1 garlic clove, crushed

2 tbsp Sichuan crispy chilli oil (see page 133)

60 ml (¼ cup) room-temperature water

First prepare the noodles. Boil a kettle of water, place the noodles in a heatproof bowl and pour the hot water over the noodles. Leave to steep for 1 minute, then stir gently to loosen and separate the noodles before draining them. Shake off excess water and set aside to cool to room temperature.

Next make the sesame dressing. Put all of the ingredients except for the water in a bowl and stir to combine; the mixture will be very thick and dry. Add 1 tablespoon of water at a time, stirring after each addition, until the mixture is smooth and creamy, and runny but not thin.

Just before serving, place the noodles, peanuts and spring onions in a large bowl. Pour the dressing over the noodles and toss until well coated. Divide among serving bowls, and top with the cucumber, sesame seeds, extra peanuts and a drizzle of chilly oil if you like it spicy.

NOTE: This recipe uses hokkien noodles that come pre-steamed and sealed in a packet. You can substitute these noodles with any chewy egg noodle or even spaghetti. Try to avoid noodles that are too thin as they will become soggy.

Tahini can be substituted for Chinese sesame paste, though the latter is very thick and dry compared to tahini. If using tahini, then omit or use less water in the dressing.

Cold skin noodles come from China's Shaanxi province, where this dish is a popular street food. With a texture all their own, *liangpi* are springy and chewy, produced by washing dough and using its starch to create these wide, flat noodles. There's no one way to cook this dish, but it's served cold and is always delicious.

SERVES 2–3

400 g (2⅔) plain (all-purpose) flour

1 tsp salt

750 ml (3 cups) water

1 tsp baking powder

sesame oil, to brush on noodles

60 ml (¼ cup) chilled water

1 carrot, julienned

1 short cucumber, julienned

1 bunch coriander (cilantro) leaves and stems, roughly chopped, to garnish (optional)

50 g (1¾ oz) Roasted peanuts (see page 133), to garnish (optional)

Sichuan crispy chilli oil (see page 133), to taste

sesame paste (or tahini), to taste

GARLIC WATER

250 ml (1 cup) water

2 star anise

1 tsp Sichuan peppercorns

3 garlic cloves, minced

1 tsp sesame oil

pinch of salt

VINEGAR WATER

125 ml (½ cup) Chinese black vinegar

125 ml (½ cup) water

1 tsp granulated sugar

Whisk the flour and salt in a bowl. Stir while pouring 250 ml (1 cup) of water into the mixture until combined. Knead into a rough dough, cover and let rest for 1 hour.

Pour the remaining water over the dough and knead until the water is very cloudy. Pour the water into a mixing bowl through a sieve, and repeat until the dough is a stretchy ball of gluten, the water almost clear. Set the dough aside. Place the water in the fridge overnight, or for at least 4 hours.

Prepare a steamer over low heat. Add the baking powder to the dough and knead for a minute to combine. Flatten the dough to about 1 cm (½ in) and place on the plate. Steam the dough for 20 minutes. Remove and let cool to room temperature. Cut the dough into bite-sized pieces. Set aside.

Once the water and starch is separated, slowly pour the water out. Using a ladle, scrape the starch at the bottom of the bowl and stir until homogenised like pancake batter.

Prepare a large bowl of iced water and set aside. Bring a large pot of water to a simmer over medium heat. Brush sesame oil on the bottom and side of a 20 cm (8-in) round baking pan. Stir the batter and pour about ¾ ladleful onto the pan, spreading evenly. Lower the pan to float on the simmering water and cover. Steam the batter until translucent, about 90 seconds. Remove the pan and float it on the iced water. Once cooled, gently peel the sheet off and transfer to a plate. Brush with sesame oil evenly. Repeat this process until all the batter is used. Roll each sheet into a roll and cut into 1 cm (½ in) strips. Set aside.

To make the garlic water, put the water, star anise and peppercorns in a small saucepan and bring to the boil over high heat. Once boiling, reduce the heat to low and simmer for 5 minutes. Add the garlic, salt and sesame oil in a heatproof bowl and stir to mix well. Pour the water through a sieve over the garlic mixture, stir and set aside to cool.

To make the vinegar water, put the ingredients in a bowl and stir to combine.

To serve, divide the noodles between serving bowls, top with a handful of carrot, cucumber, and gluten pieces. Drizzle with a few spoons of garlic and vinegar water, and add chilli oil to taste.

SUDACHI SOMEN

Chilled somen noodles with a layer of thinly sliced citrus is a dish created for Japan's hotter months. These acidic and slightly sweet noodles are prepared with *sudachi* – a citrus used for its sour notes – but yuzus and lemons can be swapped in if you can't find the Japanese fruit. While it won't be a true *sudachi somen*, it'll still be delicious.

SERVES 2

2 bundles (180 g/6½ oz) dry somen noodles

2–3 sudachi citrus, finely sliced

3-4 perilla leaves, finely chopped

125 ml (½ cup) Mentsuyu, chilled (see page 136)

500 ml (2 cups) Dashi, chilled (see page 136)

shichimi togarashi, to taste

Prepare a bowl of iced water. Bring a medium saucepan of water to the boil over high heat. Cook the noodles according to the instructions on the packet. Drain and quickly dunk the noodles into the iced water, chilling for 1 minute. Drain the noodles again and shake off excess water.

Divide the noodles between serving bowls. Place the citrus slices and a small handful of perilla leaf on top of the noodles.

Mix the mentsuyu with the dashi, then pour the chilled broth over the noodles. Sprinkle with a smidgen of shichimi togarashi, if using, and serve.

ZARU SOBA

Cold soba gets down to what we're here for: noodles, and almost nothing but the noodles. Served cold, soba noodles are dipped into a dashi-based sauce and eaten. The noodle is the true star of the show here – as it should be.

SERVES 2

2 bundles (200 g/7 oz) dried soba noodles (see Note)

2 spring (green) onions, finely sliced

a handful nori seaweed flakes

DIPPING SAUCE

2 tsp grated daikon (white radish)

2 tbsp Mentsuyu (see page 136)

90 ml (3 fl oz) iced water or Dashi (page 136)

Prepare a large bowl of iced water and set aside.

Bring a saucepan of water to a rolling boil over high heat. Cook the noodles according to the packet instructions, stirring occasionally. Drain the noodles and then rinse them under cold running water for 20 seconds. Transfer the noodles to the iced water and chill for 1 minute. Drain, shake off any excess water and set aside.

Next make the dipping sauce. Place a teaspoon of grated daikon in each serving bowl. In a third bowl combine the mentsuyu and water or dashi, then pour half into each bowl.

Place each serving of the soba noodles on a bamboo mat set on a plate, and garnish them with spring onion and nori flakes. Serve with the dipping sauce on the side.

NOTE: Sometimes a single bundle of soba is not enough for those with a big appetite! If this is the case, try using two different types of soba (original and matcha) per serving.

Dipping ramen is similar to *Zaru soba* (see page 90): a Japanese dish that consists of cold noodles that are, you guessed it, dipped. In this case, it's into piping-hot soup filled with pork belly, mushrooms, egg and fish cakes. *Tsukemen*'s soup has a salty, intense kick that hits just right when it's absorbed by the noodles.

SERVES 2

340 g (12 oz) fresh or parboiled ramen noodles

2 soft-boiled eggs (see page 61)

4 slices narutomaki fish cake

a handful bonito flakes (optional)

DIPPING SAUCE

1 tbsp vegetable oil

2 tsp grated ginger

3 garlic cloves, crushed

250 g (9 oz) pork belly, thinly sliced

80 ml (⅓ cup) Mentsuyu (see page 136)

250 ml (1 cup) water

1 tsp red miso paste

1 tsp light soy sauce

2 fresh shiitake mushrooms, finely sliced

1 bunch (50 g/1¾ oz) shimeji mushrooms

2 spring (green) onions, finely sliced, plus extra to garnish

2 tbsp Japanese rice wine vinegar

2 tsp sesame oil

Heat the oil in a medium saucepan over medium–high heat. Add the ginger and garlic, and stir-fry until fragrant, about 20 seconds. Add the pork and cook, stirring, until no longer pink, about 2 minutes. Add the mentsuyu, water, miso paste and soy sauce and stir to mix well. Bring to a boil, then reduce the heat to medium–low and simmer for 10 minutes. Skim off any impurities and foam floating on top with a fine-mesh sieve. Add the mushrooms and spring onion, stir and simmer for another 5 minutes. Add the rice wine vinegar and sesame oil, stir to mix and turn off the heat. Cover with a lid to keep warm.

Prepare a large bowl of iced water and set aside.

Bring a large saucepan of water to a rolling boil over high heat. Cook the ramen noodles according to the packet instructions, stirring occasionally with chopsticks to loosen them up. Drain and rinse the noodles under cold running water for 30 seconds, then drop in the iced water for a minute. Drain and shake off any excess water.

Divide the noodles between serving bowls. Cut each egg in half, and place two halves and two slices of the fish cake on top of the noodles in each bowl. Pour the pork and mushroom dipping sauce in another serving bowl, and garnish with the extra spring onion and the bonito flakes, if using. Serve the cold noodles with the hot dipping sauce on the side.

TSUKEMEN

HIYASHI CHUKA

Craving ramen but don't want to stand over a hot stove? Chilled ramen will save you from heating up the kitchen. The stove only turns on for the egg and noodles, which means you can spend more time enjoying the rainbow of toppings and the sweet soy sauce dressing.

SERVES 2

2 large eggs

2 tsp caster (superfine) sugar

pinch of salt

1 tbsp vegetable oil

240 g (8½ oz) fresh ramen noodles

1 short cucumber, julienned

4 ham slices, cut into thin strips

4 Japanese crab sticks, torn into thin strips

1 tomato, cut into thin wedges

1 tsp Japanese or English hot mustard (optional)

20 g (¾ oz) Japanese pickled red ginger (optional)

1 tsp toasted sesame seeds (optional)

DRESSING

1 tsp finely grated ginger

2 tbsp soy sauce

2 tbsp Japanese rice vinegar

2 tbsp water

½ tbsp caster (superfine) sugar

2 tsp sesame oil

First make the dressing. Place all of the ingredients in a mixing bowl and stir until the sugar has dissolved. Transfer the bowl to the fridge and chill for at least an hour.

Whisk the eggs, sugar and salt in a medium bowl until combined. Heat the oil in a large non-stick frying pan over medium heat. Pour the egg mixture into the pan and swirl to spread into a thin layer, cooking until the egg is set on top, about 1 minute. Flip the egg over and cook the other side for about 1 minute. Transfer the omelette to a chopping board to cool. Cut into strips 5 cm wide (2 in), stack them up, then cut crosswise into thin strips. Transfer to a plate and set aside.

Prepare a large bowl of iced water and set aside.

Bring a large saucepan of water to a rolling boil over high heat. Cook the noodles according to the packet instructions. Drain the noodles, then quickly drop them into the iced water and leave to chill for 1 minute. Drain and shake off excess water.

Divide the noodles between serving bowls. Top the noodles with the egg, cucumber, ham, crab sticks and wedges of tomato. Pour about 125 ml (½ cup) of the dressing over the noodles.

If you like, serve with hot mustard and pickled red ginger on the side, and sprinkle with sesame seeds.

MUL NAENGMYEON

Chilled buckwheat noodle soup is tart, tangy, and cold enough to get you through the hottest summer's day. In Korea, this dish of chilled beef broth and chewy buckwheat noodles is eaten as a refreshing way to cool down. But if you'd like to turn up the spice levels, check out *Bibim naengmyeon* (page 101).

SERVES 4

1 × 624 g (1 lb 6 oz) packet dried naengmyeon buckwheat noodles

Oijang-ajji (Pickled cucumber) (see page 131)

Musaengchae (Pickled radish) (see page 131)

2 hard-boiled eggs, halved and chilled

hot English mustard, to serve

BEEF BROTH

300 g (10½ oz) beef brisket

½ onion, halved

1 green apple, halved

5 garlic cloves, peeled

2 cm (¾ in) piece of ginger, finely sliced

1 tsp black peppercorns

2 spring (green) onions, white parts only

1 tsp salt

SOUP BASE

2 tbsp soy sauce

125 ml (½ cup) white vinegar

60 g (2 oz) caster (superfine) sugar

3 tsp salt

To make the beef broth, combine all the ingredients in a large stockpot. Add 3 litres (3 quarts) water and bring to the boil over high heat. Skim off any impurities that rise to the surface, then reduce the heat to medium–low. Cover with a lid (leaving it slightly ajar) and simmer for 1 hour or until the beef is tender. Remove the beef from the stock and allow the beef and stock to cool to room temperature. Wrap the beef in plastic wrap and chill in the fridge for at least 4 hours, or preferably overnight.

Strain the broth through a fine-mesh sieve into a large airtight container. Add all the ingredients for the soup base and stir until the sugar has dissolved. The soup should taste sharp, tart and mildly sweet. Taste and adjust the seasoning if necessary. Seal the container with a lid, and transfer to the fridge to chill for at least 4 hours, or preferably overnight. To speed up the chilling process, you can place the stock in the freezer for 1–2 hours, until it becomes slushy but not frozen.

Take the beef out of the fridge and slice it thinly against the grain.

Cook the buckwheat noodles according to the packet instructions. Prepare an ice bath while the noodles are cooking. Once cooked, drain the noodles and immediately plunge them into the iced water to stop the cooking process. Drain, and divide the noodles among four serving bowls.

To each bowl, add some pickled cucumber and radish, a few slices of beef and half a boiled egg. Divide the chilled soup among the bowls. Serve cold with hot mustard.

NOTE: You can also add a few slices of nashi or Asian pear if they are in season.

BIBIM GUKSU

While Spicy mixed noodles may not look all that different from *Bibim naengmyeon* (page 101), there's a key difference: the noodles. This dish trades buckwheat noodles in for wheat for a change of texture and it is typically vegetarian.

SERVES 2

200 g (7 oz) thin wheat flour noodles (somyeon)

75 g (½ cup) cabbage kimchi, finely chopped

½ short cucumber, julienned

1 hard-boiled egg, halved

toasted sesame seeds, to garnish

SPICY SAUCE

60 ml (¼ cup) kimchi juice

2 tbsp gochujang (Korean chilli paste)

1 garlic clove, finely chopped

2 tsp sesame oil

2 tsp white vinegar

1 tbsp caster (superfine) sugar

1 tbsp toasted sesame seeds

To make the spicy sauce, combine all the ingredients in a bowl and mix until the sugar has dissolved. Refrigerate until ready to use.

Prepare a large bowl of iced water and set aside.

Bring a large saucepan of water to the boil over high heat. Cook the wheat flour noodles according to the packet instructions. Drain, then immediately refresh the noodles in the iced water to stop the cooking process. Leave to chill for 2–3 minutes. Briefly stir the noodles around in the water to loosen them up, then drain.

Transfer the noodles to a large bowl, add the kimchi and spicy sauce and toss until the noodles are well coated in the sauce. Divide the noodles between two serving bowls. Top with the cucumber, half a hard-boiled egg, and sprinkle with sesame seeds to garnish. Serve immediately.

NOTE: You can make *Bibim guksu* more substantial by adding lettuce leaves, finely sliced carrot or shredded cabbage.

A sister to *Mul naengmyeon* (page 96), Spicy cold buckwheat noodles is a summer dish for spice lovers. Coated in sauce made with *gochujang*, a popular Korean condiment, these noodles will wake you up when the heat's got you drowsy.

SERVES 4

1 × 624 g (1 lb 6 oz) packet dried naengmyeon buckwheat noodles

Oijang-ajji (Pickled cucumber) (see page 131)

Musaengchae (Pickled radish) (see page 131)

2 hard-boiled eggs, halved and chilled

toasted sesame seeds, to garnish

BEEF BROTH

300 g (10½ oz) beef brisket

½ onion, halved

1 green apple, halved

5 garlic cloves, peeled

2 cm (¾ in) piece ginger, finely sliced

1 tsp whole black peppercorns

2 spring (green) onions, white parts only

1 tsp salt

SPICY SAUCE

½ nashi or Asian pear, cored

½ onion, peeled

60 ml (¼ cup) beef broth

2 garlic cloves, grated

20 g (¼ cup) gochugaru (Korean chilli flakes)

2 tbsp gochujang (Korean chilli paste)

1 tbsp caster (superfine) sugar

1 tbsp fish sauce

2 tbsp white vinegar

2 tsp sesame oil

To make the beef broth, combine all the ingredients in a large stockpot. Add 3 litres (3 quarts) water and bring to the boil over high heat. Skim off any impurities that rise to the surface, then reduce the heat to medium–low. Cover with a lid (leaving it slightly ajar), and simmer for 1 hour, until the beef is tender. Remove the beef from the stock and set aside to cool to room temperature. Wrap the beef in plastic wrap and chill in the fridge for at least 4 hours, or preferably overnight.

Strain the broth through a fine-mesh sieve into a large airtight container. Reserve 60 ml (¼ cup) of the broth to make the sauce. You can discard the rest of the broth or keep it to make Mul naengmyeon (page 96).

To make the spicy sauce, combine all the ingredients in a food processor and blend to a fine purée. Refrigerate until needed.

Take the beef out of the fridge and slice it thinly against the grain.

Cook the noodles according to the packet instructions. Prepare an ice bath while the noodles are cooking. Once cooked, drain the noodles and immediately plunge them into the iced water to stop the cooking process. Drain, and place the noodles in a bowl.

Add the spicy sauce and toss until all the noodles are well coated. Divide the noodles among four serving bowls and top each with some pickled cucumber and radish, a few slices of beef and half a boiled egg. Sprinkle sesame seeds over the top and serve.

This noodle salad combines grilled, crispy pork, aromatic herbs and fresh vegetables on a bed of rice vermicelli. A South Vietnamese–style dish, with flavours that will make this a go-to on hot days (or anytime you want something refreshing and delicious).

SERVES 4

600 g (1 lb 5 oz) boneless pork shoulder, thinly sliced

200 g (7 oz) vermicelli bun (rice noodles)

½ butter (Bibb) lettuce, shredded (optional)

2 short cucumbers, Julienned

150 g (5½ oz) Pickled carrot and daikon (see page 131)

2 tbsp Fried shallots (see page 133)

80 ml (⅓ cup) Spring onion oil (see page 134)

1 bunch mint, leaves picked, to garnish

1 bunch Vietnamese mint, leaves picked, to garnish

100 g (3½ oz) Roasted peanuts (see page 133), to serve

Nuoc mam dipping sauce (see page 134), to serve

MARINADE

2 shallots, finely chopped

2 garlic cloves, finely chopped

1 tbsp honey

3 tbsp fish sauce

3 tbsp vegetable oil

1 tbsp caster (superfine) sugar

Combine the marinade ingredients in a large bowl and stir until the sugar and honey have dissolved. Add the pork and mix well. Set aside in the fridge to marinate for at least 4 hours, or preferably overnight.

Prepare a charcoal grill or preheat a barbecue grill to medium–high.

Cook the noodles according to the packet instructions, then drain and run under cold water until cool. Drain again and set aside.

When the charcoal grill is ready (the embers should be glowing red with a small flame on the charcoal), place the pork on the grill and cook, turning frequently, for 8–10 minutes until golden brown. Transfer to a plate.

Divide the noodles among four bowls and add the lettuce (if using), cucumber and pickles. Top with the pork and fried shallots and drizzle over the spring onion oil. Garnish with a handful of herbs and serve with the peanuts and nuoc mam on the side, to add as desired.

YUM WOONSEN

Yum woonsen, Thai glass noodle salad, has many variations. This recipe uses minced (ground) pork, but seafood is also very common in Thailand. A dish that's perfect to share, *Yum woonsen* is a light, fresh way to enjoy noodles that doesn't take long to prepare.

SERVES 4

250 g (9 oz) dried glass noodles

3 tbsp vegetable oil, for frying

4 garlic cloves, finely chopped

25 g (1 oz) dried shrimp

100 g (3½ oz) minced (ground) pork

3½ tbsp fish sauce

¼ red onion, finely sliced

3½ tbsp lime juice

1½ tsp caster (superfine) sugar

2 tbsp sliced red bird's eye chillies

small handful roughly chopped coriander (cilantro) leaves and stems, to garnish

small handful roughly chopped spring (green) onion, to garnish

25 g (1 oz) Roasted peanuts (see page 133), to garnish

Fill a large bowl with cold water and soak the glass noodles until softened. Drain in a colander and fill the bowl with iced water. Bring a saucepan of water to the boil over high heat and blanch the noodles for 10–20 seconds. Using tongs, transfer the noodles to the iced water to stop the cooking process. Once cool, drain and set aside.

Heat the oil in a non-stick frying pan over medium heat and sauté the garlic for 4–5 minutes, until golden. Remove from the oil with a slotted spoon and set aside to drain on paper towel. Fry the dried shrimp in the same oil for 2–3 minutes, until crisp. Remove from the oil and set aside to drain on paper towel. Reserve the oil and allow to cool to room temperature.

Bring a small saucepan of water to the boil over high heat and cook the pork, stirring constantly to break it apart, for 2–3 minutes, until no more pink remains. Drain most of the water off, return the saucepan to the stove and reduce the heat to medium. Add 1 tablespoon of the fish sauce and sauté the pork for 2 minutes, then remove from the heat and set aside to cool.

Combine the noodles, fried garlic, reserved oil, fried shrimp, red onion and pork mince in a large non-reactive bowl and mix well. Season with the remaining fish sauce, the lime juice, caster sugar and chillies, adjusting the balance of flavours to your liking, if necessary.

Transfer to a serving plate and garnish with coriander, spring onion and roasted peanuts.

TOMATO EGG NOODLES

A recipe that's a testament that you don't need a full pantry to make a delicious meal. Tomatoes, eggs and noodles are a classic Chinese combination that appears in countless variations, for good reason. It's simple, it's easy, and the ingredients may already be in your kitchen.

SERVES 1

150 g (5½) fresh Shanghai lamian noodles (see Note)

1 tsp sesame oil

2 tbsp vegetable oi

3 eggs, beaten with a pinch of salt

1 garlic clove, finely chopped

1 tomato, diced

½ tbsp light soy sauce

1 tsp dark soy sauce

1 tsp ground white pepper

1 tsp chicken bouillon

125 ml (½ cup) water

1 spring (green) onion, green part only, finely sliced

Bring a saucepan of water to a rolling boil over high heat. Cook the noodles for 2 minutes, drain and transfer to a serving bowl. Drizzle with the sesame oil, stir well and set aside.

Heat 1 tablespoon of the vegetable oil in a non-stick frying pan over high heat until smoking hot. Pour the beaten eggs into the pan, stir with a spatula and as the egg cooks, separate it into big chunks. Cook for another minute, then transfer to a plate and set aside.

In the same pan, heat the remaining oil over medium–high heat. Add the garlic and stir-fry for 15 seconds, then add tomato and stir-fry until it softens, about a minute. Add the light and dark soy sauces, white pepper and chicken bouillon, stir-frying for 10 seconds to mix well. Add the egg and water, stir occasionally and let simmer until the sauce thickens, about 2 minutes.

Pour the tomato egg sauce over the noodles and garnish with spring onion to serve.

NOTE: Shanghai *lamian* is a thick white wheat noodle, available at Asian supermarkets, but any thick white noodles will work.

S A C H A B E E F N O O D L E S

If you ever find yourself in a Hong Kong cafe, this dish is one of the most popular items to order. Made with a Hong Kong–style satay sauce, these noodles are enjoyed by Hongkongers for breakfast, but they also make a great quick lunch.

SERVES 4

300 g (10½ oz) beef tenderloin (or any cut for quick cooking), cut into thin strips

100 g (⅓ cup) sa cha sauce (see Note)

1 tsp caster (superfine) sugar

3 tbsp canola oil (or other cooking oil)

1 garlic clove, finely chopped

1 red shallot, finely chopped

340 g (12 oz) instant noodles

1 spring (green) onion, finely sliced

toasted sesame seeds, to garnish

MARINADE

1 tbsp light soy sauce

1 tsp caster (superfine) sugar

2 tsp cornflour (cornstarch)

1 tbsp canola oil

To make the marinade, combine all the ingredients and 2 tablespoons of water in a bowl. Add the beef and turn to coat well, then set aside to marinate for 30 minutes.

In a small bowl, combine the sa cha sauce, sugar and 125 ml (½ cup) water.

Heat a frying pan over high heat. Add 1 tablespoon of the oil, then the beef and sauté for 2 minutes or until just starting to brown. Transfer the beef to a bowl and set aside.

Wipe out the pan and return to high heat. Heat the remaining oil, then add the garlic and shallot and sauté for 30 seconds. Add the beef, followed by the sauce mixture. Reduce the heat to low and cook for about 2 minutes, until heated through and the beef has had time to absorb the flavour.

Meanwhile, cook the noodles according to the packet instructions. Drain.

Divide the noodles among serving bowls and top with the beef and sauce. Scatter over the spring onion and sesame seeds to serve.

NOTE: Sa cha sauce, the star of this dish, is available in Asian supermarkets.

Koreans are not the only ones to have realised that instant noodles and SPAM are meant to be. While you can have *Gong zai mein* at any time of the day, this is another popular breakfast dish in Hong Kong, complete with a fried egg, sunny side up. A simple dish that features processed foods at their best.

SERVES 1

2 tsp vegetable oil

tinned SPAM, cut into 0.5 cm (⅓ in) slices

1 large egg

1 packet chicken-flavoured instant noodles

1 spring (green) onion, green part only, finely sliced

sesame oil, to taste

ground white pepper, to taste

Heat the oil in a frying pan over medium heat and fry the SPAM slices on both sides until golden and crispy around the edges. Remove the SPAM and set aside.

In the same pan, fry the egg over medium–low heat, sunny side up for about 3 minutes. Turn heat off, put the SPAM back in the pan with the egg and keep warm.

Bring 500 ml (2 cups) of water to a rolling boil over high heat. Add the noodles and sachet of seasoning and cook for 2 minutes, stirring occasionally to loosen the noodles.

Pour the noodles and broth into a serving bowl, and drape the SPAM and egg over the top. Garnish with the spring onion, add a dash of sesame oil and sprinkle with a smidgen of pepper to serve.

GONG ZAI MEIN

ABURA SOBA

A dish with a trick up its sleeve: despite what 'soba' suggests, it is made with ramen noodles. The other part of its name, *abura*, means oil in Japanese. That's because there's no broth here. This is a soupless ramen, and for those in a hurry, it can be dressed down without the chashu (see Note).

SERVES 2

1 soft-boiled egg, halved (see page 61)

300 g (10½ oz) fresh ramen noodles

1 spring (green) onion, green part only, finely sliced

a handful nori seaweed flakes

10 slices menma (fermented bamboo shoots) (optional)

chilli oil, to taste

ROASTED CHASHU

2 pieces pork spare ribs

3 tbsp soy sauce

1 tbsp sweet mirin

1 tbsp sake

2 tsp sugar

1 garlic clove, smashed

TARE

1 tbsp Japanese rice wine vinegar

2 tsp red miso paste

2 tbsp sesame oil

To make the chashu, place all the ingredients in a zip lock bag and massage the pork until well coated. Set aside and marinate for at least 1 hour.

Preheat the oven to 180ºC (350ºF). Place the pork ribs on a wire rack over a baking tray, reserving the remaining marinade for later. Roast the pork for 30 minutes, then turn over and roast for another 20 minutes. Remove the pork ribs from the oven, set aside and keep warm.

To make the tare, place the leftover marinade in a small saucepan, add the rice wine vinegar and miso paste, and whisk to combine. Bring to the boil over medium heat, then simmer for 1 minute until the liquid has reduced by half and thickened. Divide the tare sauce between two serving bowls, then add 1 tablespoon of sesame oil to each bowl.

Bring a saucepan of water to a rolling boil over high heat. Tease the ramen noodles apart, then drop them in the hot water, stirring occasionally with chopsticks. Cook according to the packet instructions. Drain and shake off excess water. Divide the noodles between the bowls with the tare sauce. Toss the noodles until well coated.

Top the noodles with a pork rib, half a soft-boiled egg, spring onions, nori, bamboo shoots and a dash of chilli oil.

NOTE: You can make this dish instant by serving it with store-bought toppings of your choice, like fried tofu puffs or fish cakes.

C H E E S E   R A M E N

Cheese? On ramen?? While this combination may make the uninitiated pause, cheesy ramen is not a new creation. It is, rather, a marriage of gooey, melted cheese, butter and instant noodles, whipped up into the perfect bowl of comfort food.

SERVES 1

1 packet Shin Ramyun instant noodles (comes with dehydrated vegetables and chilli powder sachets)

1 tbsp (14 g) butter

50 ml (1¾ fl oz) full-cream milk

2 slices American cheese (or cheddar)

2 tsp finely grated parmesan

1 spring (green) onion, green part only, finely sliced

Bring a small saucepan or pot of water to a rolling boil over high heat. Add the instant noodles and the dehydrated vegetables in the sachet. Cook the noodles according to the packet instructions. Drain the noodles through a mesh strainer, reserving 2 tablespoons of the cooking water, and set aside.

Heat a non-stick frying pan over medium heat. Add the butter, then stir until melted and bubbling. Add the milk and give it a quick stir. Place the cheese slices in the pan and sprinkle in the chilli powder from the sachet. When the milk starts bubbling again, stir continuously until all the cheese has melted to become a thick creamy sauce. Add the noodles to the sauce and stir well until the noodles are well coated in the cheese sauce. Add the reserved water and quickly stir.

Transfer the cheese ramen to a serving bowl. Sprinkle with parmesan, then garnish with spring onion.

If you want ramyeon (and we *actually* mean ramyeon), you don't need a huge budget. You can dress these noodles up as much, or as little, as you want – they're delicious as they are. Ramyeon, unlike ramen, is always made with instant noodles and it is usually spicier.

SERVES 1

1 packet instant noodles (see Note)

1 garlic clove, minced

1 tsp sesame oil

1 tsp gochugaru (Korean chilli powder), plus extra (optional)

1 fresh shiitake mushroom, finely sliced

1 large egg

1 spring (green) onion, finely sliced

150 g (¼) cup kimchi

Add 550 ml (18½ fl oz) of water to a small saucepan and bring to the boil over medium–high heat. If the instant noodles come with a sachet of dehydrated vegetables, add it now, together with the sachet of seasoning. Once boiling, add the instant noodles and cook for 1 minute. Stir to loosen the noodles, then add the garlic, sesame oil, gochugaru and mushroom and cook for another minute.

Crack the egg on top of the noodles, reduce the heat to medium and cook for 30 seconds. Turn off the heat, top with the spring onion and kimchi, and serve in the saucepan.

NOTE: You can use any type of instant ramen noodles for this recipe.

JJAPAGURI

If you've seen *Parasite*, you've seen *Jjapaguri*. This dish features not one, but two types of instant noodles – Chapagetti and Neoguri. Prepared with steak and coated in a sauce that's a blend of seasonings (Chapagetti's is sweet and Neoguri's is spicy), this fusion is worthy of the silver screen.

SERVES 2

200 g (7 oz) beef sirloin steak

salt and pepper, to taste

1 tbsp vegetable oil

2 garlic cloves, finely chopped

1 packet Chapagetti instant noodles

1 packet Neoguri instant noodles

50 g (1¾ oz) short cucumber, julienned, to serve

2 tbsp danmuji (Korean yellow pickled radish), to serve (optional)

Cut the beef into bite-sized pieces and season with salt and pepper.

Add 1.5 litres (1.5 quarts) of water to a medium saucepan and bring to the boil over medium–high heat.

In the meantime, heat the oil in a frying pan over medium–high heat, and add the garlic. Stir-fry for 10 seconds, then add the beef and cook until browned on all sides and still medium-rare on the inside, about 2 minutes.

Once the water is boiling, add the noodles and dehydrated vegetable mix from the packets and cook for 3 minutes, stirring occasionally.

The noodles and beef will be ready at the same time. Transfer the noodles and a cup of the boiling water to the pan with the steak. Turn the heat to medium–low, then add the Chapagetti seasoning and the Neoguri seasoning. Stir until all the noodles are well coated in the seasonings and the sauce has thickened slightly.

Add the oil from the Chapagetti and more water if you like it 'saucy', then stir and transfer to serving bowls. Garnish with the cucumber and pickled radish.

KOREAN FIRE NOODLES

A glass of milk is not necessary to prepare these noodles, but it is advisable to have one on hand while eating. This dish is for chilli fanatics who love a dish that makes them sweat. Don't say we didn't warn you ...

SERVES 2

2 packets instant ramen or udon noodles

large handful shredded iceberg lettuce leaves (optional)

fried shallots, to garnish

2 eggs, fried sunny side up

glasses of milk, on standby

FIRE NOODLE SAUCE

1 tbsp vegetable oil

2 tbsp gochujang (Korean chilli paste)

2 tsp Korean capsaicin hot sauce (see Note)

2 tbsp light soy sauce

1 tbsp dark soy sauce

2 tsp rice vinegar

3 garlic cloves, crushed

2.5 cm (1 in) piece ginger, grated

2 tsp sesame oil

1 tbsp caster (superfine) sugar

To make the fire noodle sauce, combine the ingredients in a bowl and stir until the sugar has dissolved. Set aside.

Cook the noodles according to the packet instructions, then drain, saving 125 ml (½ cup) of the cooking water. Divide the noodles between two serving bowls.

Add 2 tablespoons of the fire noodle sauce to each bowl and toss until the noodles are well coated. Top with the shredded lettuce, if using, and fried shallots, and finish with the fried eggs.

Serve with glasses of milk to reduce the burn!

NOTE: Korean capsaicin is a spice enhancer with a Scoville Heat Scale of over 15,000,000! So you only need a little to feel the burn. It can be purchased from any Asian supermarket.

A hotpot for spice lovers who want to warm up in the winter. Army base stew's origins lie with the end of the Korean War, when surplus food from US army bases collided with Korean kitchens. The result? A delicious cultural fusion of SPAM and kimchi.

SERVES 4–6

200 g (1 cup) kimchi, roughly chopped

200 g (7 oz) SPAM, thinly sliced

2 Frankfurt sausages, sliced diagonally

300 g (10½ oz) firm tofu, sliced into 1 cm (½ in) thick strips (optional)

200 g (7 oz) shiitake mushrooms, finely sliced

50 g (1¾ oz) enoki mushrooms, roots trimmed

50 g (1¾ oz) frozen tteok (Korean tubular rice cakes; see Note), soaked in warm water for 20 minutes, drained

1 litre (4 cups) vegetable stock

2 spring (green) onions, green parts only, finely sliced

110 g (4 oz) instant ramen noodles

1–2 slices stretchy cheese, such as American yellow

steamed rice, to serve

BUDAE JJIGAE CHILLI PASTE

3 garlic cloves, crushed

2 tbsp gochugaru (Korean chilli flakes)

1 tbsp gochujang (Korean chilli paste)

2 tbsp mirin

1 tbsp soy sauce

1 tsp sesame oil

2 tsp granulated sugar

To make the budae jjigae chilli paste, combine the ingredients in a bowl. Set aside.

Arrange the kimchi, SPAM, sausage, tofu, if using, mushrooms and tteok around the base of a shallow flameproof casserole dish. Spoon the chilli paste into the centre of the dish, then pour the vegetable stock around the chilli paste. Cover, bring to the boil over medium–high heat and cook for 5–8 minutes.

Gently stir the chilli paste into the broth and scatter the spring onion over the top. Place the ramen noodles in the dish, then place the cheese slices on top of the noodles. Let the stew simmer for 2–3 minutes, until the noodles are cooked. Remove from the heat and take the dish to the table.

If you have a portable gas burner, serve the hot stew over the burner at the table so it remains steaming hot.

Serve the stew with steamed rice to soak up that spicy sauce.

NOTE: Frozen *tteok* can be purchased from Asian supermarkets.

CHASHU PORK

MAKES 8 PORTIONS

1 kg (2 lb 3 oz) boneless pork belly, skin on

250 ml (1 cup) sake

250 ml (1 cup) mirin

125 ml (½ cup) soy sauce

115 g (½ cup) caster (superfine) sugar

4 spring (green) onions, quartered

2 shallots, halved

6 garlic cloves, smashed

20 g (¾ oz) ginger, sliced

Preheat the oven to 135°C (275°F).

Roll up the pork belly with the skin on the outside and tie with kitchen string at 2 cm (¾ in) intervals along the pork.

Place the remaining ingredients and 500 ml (2 cups) of water in a Dutch oven and bring to the boil. Remove from the heat and add the pork. Cover and transfer to the oven for 4–5 hours, turning the pork occasionally, until completely cooked through and tender.

Cool the pork and the liquid to room temperature, then cover, and transfer the lot to the fridge and leave to rest overnight to achieve maximum flavour.

Remove the pork from the liquid and thinly slice. Serve the chashu on your ramen of choice.

The liquid can be used as the Ajitsuke Tamago marinade (see page 130) or as a tare seasoning for your ramen.

The sliced chashu and liquid will keep in airtight containers in the fridge for 5–6 days.

SOY-MARINATED BARBECUED BEEF

BULGOGI

SERVES 2–4

300 g (10½ oz) beef tenderloin or rib eye (see Note)

½ onion, sliced (optional)

1 spring (green) onion, cut into 5 cm (2 in) lengths

MARINADE

2 garlic cloves, crushed

1 tbsp caster (superfine) sugar

2 tbsp soy sauce

1 tbsp mirin

2 tsp sesame oil

1 pinch freshly ground black pepper

Cut the beef in half lengthways into two long strips, then slice each half against the grain into 3 mm (⅛ in) thick slices. Combine the beef slices, onion, if using, and spring onion in a large bowl and set aside.

To make the marinade, put all the ingredients in a bowl and stir until the sugar has dissolved. Pour the marinade over the beef and, using your hands (wear food preparation gloves if necessary), mix until well combined. Cover with plastic wrap and leave to marinate in the fridge for at least 1 hour.

Heat your barbecue to high, or set a chargrill pan over high heat. Working in batches, chargrill the beef for 1–2 minutes on each side until caramelised.

NOTE: If you freeze the beef for about 1 hour before slicing it, it will be much easier to cut thinly.

RENDERED PORK FAT

MAKES ABOUT 260 G (1¼ CUPS)

500 g (1 lb 2 oz) organic pork fat, cut into 3 cm (1¼ in) cubes

Place the fat and 125 ml (½ cup) of water in a heavy-based saucepan and cook over low heat for 4–5 hours. Occasionally stir the fat and ensure that the heat is gentle enough to melt the fat instead of charring and burning it. During this time the water will evaporate and the fat will very slowly render into liquid, leaving behind small, golden-brown chunks of fat.

Drain the liquid through a fine-meshed sieve into a sterilised jar and discard the solids. The liquid will be a light yellowish colour but will change to pure white when solidified. Alternatively, cook the fat in a slow cooker, covered, on low for 7–8 hours.

Rendered pork fat will keep in an airtight container in the fridge for up to 3 months or in the freezer for up to 6 months. Use in ramen broths and tares, and for frying.

ONSEN TAMAGO

MAKES 4
PORTIONS

4 eggs, at room
temperature

2 tbsp mirin

1 tsp caster (superfine)
sugar

125 ml (½ cup) light soy
sauce

250 ml (1 cup) cold Dashi
(see page 136)

1 spring (green) onion,
finely sliced

Using a digital thermometer to assist you, heat a large saucepan of water to exactly 75°C (165°F). Place the eggs in the pan and cook at this temperature for 13 minutes. Transfer to an ice bath to stop the cooking process.

Meanwhile, combine the mirin, sugar and soy sauce in a saucepan over medium heat and simmer for 1–2 minutes until the sugar has dissolved.

Pour the mirin mixture into the dashi and stir to combine. Divide the liquid among four small bowls, add a peeled egg and garnish with a little spring onion. Serve alongside your ramen of choice.

AJITSUKE TAMAGO

MAKES 4
PORTIONS

4 eggs

125 ml (½ cup) soy sauce

60 ml (¼ cup) mirin

60 ml (¼ cup) sake

3 tsp caster (superfine)
sugar

1 garlic clove, smashed

Place the eggs in a saucepan of boiling water and boil for 6 minutes. Drain and plunge into an ice bath.

Meanwhile, combine the remaining ingredients in a saucepan over medium heat and simmer for 1–2 minutes until the sugar has dissolved. Remove from the heat, transfer to a heatproof bowl and set aside to cool completely.

Peel the eggs and place them in the cooled soy sauce liquid. Refrigerate for 4–5 hours and up to 12 hours. The longer you leave the eggs, the stronger the flavour will be.

Cut the eggs in half, and serve them on your ramen of choice. You can either discard the liquid or use it to season your ramen.

PICKLED CUCUMBER

MAKES ABOUT 230 G (8 OZ)

1 short cucumber

¼ tsp salt

2 tsp caster (superfine) sugar

2 tbsp white vinegar

Cut the cucumber in half lengthways, then cut each half diagonally into slices 3 mm (⅛ in) thick. Transfer to a bowl, then add the salt and sugar. Toss to combine, leave to sit for 10 minutes, then add the vinegar and mix well. Refrigerate until ready to use.

PICKLED RADISH

MAKES ABOUT 240 G (8½ OZ)

200 g (7 oz) Korean radishes, peeled

¼ tsp salt

2 tsp caster (superfine) sugar

2 tbsp white vinegar

For the pickled radish, finely slice the radishes then stack the slices and cut into strips 2 cm (¾ in) wide. Transfer to a bowl, then add the salt and sugar. Toss to combine, leave to sit for 10 minutes, then add the vinegar and mix well. Refrigerate until ready to use.

PICKLED CARROT AND DAIKON

MAKES 1.25 KG (2 LB 12 OZ)

1 kg (2 lb 3 oz) carrots, julienned

300 g (10½ oz) daikon radish, julienned

PICKLE LIQUID

150 ml (5 fl oz) white vinegar

100 g (3½ oz) caster (superfine) sugar

To make the pickle liquid, combine the vinegar and sugar in a bowl and add 100 ml (3½ fl oz) of water. Stir until the sugar has dissolved.

Rinse the carrot and daikon under warm running water for 5 minutes, then drain thoroughly and pat dry with paper towel. Transfer to a large plastic container or non-reactive bowl.

Pour the pickle liquid over the vegetables and set aside in the fridge for 2 days, after which time the pickles will be ready to use.

Pickled carrot and daikon will keep in the fridge for up to 2 weeks.

JAPANESE QUICK PICKLES

MAKES ABOUT 680 ML (23 FL OZ)

175 g (1½ cups) finely sliced radishes

1 umeboshi plum

1 small red chilli, halved

½ garlic clove, sliced (optional)

250 ml (1 cup) rice wine vinegar

2 tbsp caster (superfine) sugar

2 tsp fine sea salt

5 black peppercorns

Place the radish, plum, chilli and garlic, if using, in a heatproof bowl.

Heat the rice wine vinegar, 250 ml (1 cup) of water, sugar, salt and peppercorns in a saucepan over medium heat. Stir to dissolve the sugar and salt and bring to the boil. Pour over the sliced vegetables and leave to cool.

Serve alongside pork dishes, ramen and cold noodle salads.

The pickles will keep in an airtight container in the fridge for up to 1 week.

SEASONED ENGLISH SPINACH

SIGEUMCHI MUCHIM

SERVES 4

250–300 g (9-10½ oz) English spinach (about 1 bunch)

1 garlic clove, finely chopped

1 tsp sesame oil

1 tsp toasted sesame seeds

salt, to taste

Prepare a bowl of iced water and set aside.

Wash the spinach under cold running water to remove any dirt. Shake off any excess water, then set aside.

Bring a large saucepan of water to a rolling boil over high heat. Blanch the spinach for 30 seconds, then drain and immediately refresh in the iced water to stop the cooking process. Leave to chill in the water for 10 minutes, then drain and trim off the roots ends of the stems.

Spread the spinach out on a chopping board, then cut the stems and leaves into 5 cm (2 in) lengths. Gather the spinach with both hands and squeeze firmly to remove any excess water. Loosen up the leaves and transfer to a mixing bowl.

Add the garlic, sesame oil and sesame seeds and toss everything together with your hands. Season to taste with salt and serve right away or store in the fridge in an airtight container for up to 2 days.

FRIED SHALLOTS

**MAKES 50 G
(1³/₄ OZ)**

300 ml (10 fl oz)
vegetable oil

4 shallots, finely sliced

Heat the vegetable oil in a small saucepan to 170°C (340°F) on a kitchen thermometer.

Place the shallot in the oil and cook, stirring continuously to break up the shallot, for 7–8 minutes until golden brown.

Using a slotted spoon, remove the shallot from the oil and drain on a plate lined with paper towel. Using two forks, quickly separate and loosen the shallot – if it stays in a clump it will burn in the residual heat.

Fried shallots will keep in an airtight container for 2–3 days.

ROASTED PEANUTS

**MAKES ABOUT
100 G (3½ OZ)**

100 g (3½ oz) raw
peanuts (without skins)

Preheat the oven to 180°C (350°F).

Place the peanuts on a baking tray and roast, checking them frequently to ensure they don't burn, for 10–15 minutes until golden brown.

Allow to cool, then lightly crush.

The crushed peanuts will keep in an airtight container in the pantry for 1–2 weeks.

SICHUAN CRISPY CHILLI OIL

**MAKES ABOUT
225 ML (7½ OZ)**

60 ml (¼ cup) dried chilli
flakes

2 tbsp sesame seeds

2 tsp salt

125 ml (½ cup)
vegetable oil

2 star anise

1 teaspoon Sichuan
peppercorns

Put the chilli flakes, sesame seeds and salt in a heatproof bowl. Heat the oil, star anise and Sichuan peppercorns in a small saucepan over medium heat. When the oil starts to ripple, use a strainer to scoop out the aromatics. Pour the hot oil carefully over the chilli mixture, give it a stir and set aside to cool.

The oil will keep in an airtight container in the fridge for 2 weeks.

HOTPOT DIPPING SAUCE

MAKES ABOUT 250 ML (1 CUP)

125 ml (½ cup) hoisin sauce

80 g (2¾ oz) satay sauce (store-bought is fine)

1 tbsp sriracha chilli sauce

juice of 1 lime

Combine all the ingredients in a large bowl.

The sauce will keep in an airtight container in the fridge for 5 days.

SPRING ONION OIL

MAKES 125 ML (½ CUP)

3 spring (green) onions, finely sliced

pinch of salt

100 ml (3½ fl oz) vegetable oil

Place the spring onion and salt in a metal bowl.

Heat the vegetable oil in a small saucepan to 150°C (300°F) on a kitchen thermometer, then pour the oil over the spring onion. Stir and set aside to infuse until you are ready to use.

Spring onion oil should be used the same day it is made.

NUOC MAM DIPPING SAUCE

MAKES 600 ML (20½ FL OZ)

2 garlic cloves, finely chopped

3 bird's eye chillies, finely chopped or sliced

150 ml (5 fl oz) fish sauce

100 ml (3½ fl oz) white vinegar

140 g (5 oz) caster (superfine) sugar

Combine the ingredients and 200 ml (7 fl oz) of water in a bowl and stir until the sugar has dissolved.

Nuoc mam will keep in an airtight container in the fridge for up to 2 weeks.

LEMONGRASS SATE

MAKES ABOUT
1.75 LITRES
(60 FL OZ

6 lemongrass stalks, white part only, sliced

15 long red chillies, sliced

6 bird's eye chillies, sliced

3 onions, chopped

12 garlic cloves

1.5 litres (6 cups) vegetable oil

150 ml (5 fl oz) fish sauce

In a food processor, individually blitz the lemongrass, long red chillies, bird's eye chillies, onion and garlic.

Place the blitzed onion in a square of muslin (cheesecloth) and squeeze out and discard any excess liquid.

Heat the oil in a large saucepan over low heat to 80°C (175°F) on a kitchen thermometer. Stirring regularly throughout the whole process to avoid burning, empty the onion from the muslin into the oil and cook for 10 minutes. Add the garlic and cook for 5 minutes, then add both the chillies and cook for 20–30 minutes. Finally, add the lemongrass and fish sauce and cook for 20 minutes or until the sate is a rich red colour.

Set aside to cool completely. The sate will keep in an airtight container in the fridge for up to 6 months.

BLACK GARLIC OIL

BLACK MAYU

MAKES 160 ML
(5½ FL OZ)

80 ml (⅓ cup) peanut oil

1 garlic bulb, peeled and chopped

80 ml (⅓ cup) toasted sesame oil

1 tbsp toasted black sesame seeds

pinch of salt

Heat the peanut oil and garlic in a frying pan over medium heat. Cook slowly until the garlic starts to brown. Reduce the heat to low and continue cooking for 7–8 minutes, until the garlic blackens. Remove from the heat, add the sesame oil and process in a blender with the sesame seeds and salt until smooth. Allow to cool before straining through a fine-mesh sieve into a container.

Drizzle over your ramen of choice.

Mayu will keep in an airtight container in the fridge for 1½–2 months.

DASHI

MAKES 1 LITRE (4 CUPS)

1 piece (5 g) kombu

1 litre (4 cups) water

10 g (⅓ oz) dried bonito flakes

To make the kombu, place the kombu and water in a saucepan, turn the heat on medium–low and slowly bring to the boil, about 10 minutes. When the water is about to start boiling, remove the kombu from the water. Add the bonito flakes and bring to the boil. Reduce the heat to low, simmer for 30 seconds, then turn off the heat and leave to steep for 10 minutes. Strain the dashi through a fine-mesh sieve into a heatproof bowl.

Dash will keep in an airtight container in the fridge for up to 5 days.

MENTSUYU

MAKES ABOUT 500 ML (2 CUPS)

250 ml (1 cup) light soy sauce

250 ml (1 cup) mirin

125 ml (½ cup) sake

1 piece (5 g) kombu

1 cup dried bonito flakes

Place all the ingredients in a saucepan and slowly bring to the boil over medium–low heat. Once bubbling, reduce the heat to low and simmer for 5 minutes. Turn off the heat and let cool. Place a sheet of paper towel over a fine-mesh sieve and pass the liquid through the sieve into a container Discard the solids. Chill the mentsuyu in the fridge until ready to use.

Mentsuyu will keep in an airtight container in the fridge for up to 5 days.

VEGAN BROTH

MAKES 2 PORTIONS

800 ml (27 fl oz) Vegan stock

1 × quantity Vegan tare

VEGAN STOCK
Makes 2 litres (8 cups)

1 leek, roughly chopped

2 onions, quartered

2 carrots, roughly chopped

4 spring (green) onions

3 tsp peanut oil

6 dried shiitake mushrooms

6 garlic cloves, smashed

20 g (¾ oz) ginger, chopped

½ tsp white peppercorns

15 g (½ oz) kombu

VEGAN TARE

100 g (⅓ cup) red miso paste

2 tbsp tahini

1 tbsp soy sauce

1 tbsp mirin

1 tbsp sake

1 tbsp ponzu

2 tsp toasted sesame oil

1 garlic clove, finely grated

½ tsp finely grated ginger

To make the stock, rinse the leek to remove any grit. Transfer to a bowl along with the onion, carrot, spring onions and oil. Toss well to combine. Place in a large saucepan over medium–high heat and slightly char the vegetables to deepen their flavour. Add the mushrooms, garlic, ginger and peppercorns. Cover with 4 litres (4¼ quarts) of water and bring to the boil. Reduce to a rapid simmer and cook for 1–1½ hours until reduced to about 2 litres (2 quarts) of stock. Add the kombu, simmer for 5 minutes, then remove from the heat and leave to infuse in the stock for 15–20 minutes.

Strain the stock. Discard the remaining solids.

Leave to cool before refrigerating. The stock will keep in an airtight container in the fridge for up to 5 days or in the freezer for up to 3 months.

To make the tare, whisk the ingredients in a small bowl to combine. The tare will keep in an airtight container in the fridge for up to 5 days.

To make the broth, combine the ingredients in a saucepan and bring to a simmer.

Serve over ramen, rice or kelp noodles with your favourite toppings.

SHIO BROTH

MAKES 2 PORTIONS

400 ml (13½ fl oz) Simple chicken stock

400 ml (13½ fl oz) Dashi (see page 136)

1 × quantity Shio tare

1½ tbsp Rendered pork fat (see page 129) or chicken fat

SIMPLE CHICKEN STOCK

Makes 2 litres (2 quarts)

1 × 2 kg (4 lb 6 oz) organic whole chicken, rinsed

6 garlic cloves, smashed

½ tsp white peppercorns

SHIO TARE

2 tbsp fine sea salt

1 tbsp boiling water

2 tbsp sake

1 tbsp mirin

2 tsp toasted sesame oil

1 tsp soy sauce

1 garlic clove, finely grated

To make the stock, place the chicken in a large stockpot, cover with 5 litres (5¼ quarts) of water and slowly bring to the boil. Skim off any impurities that rise to the surface, then reduce the heat and maintain a slow simmer for about 4 hours, adding the garlic cloves and peppercorns in the final hour of cooking.

Strain the stock and pick the meat from the bones, reserving it to use in your ramen of choice or in soups or salads.

Leave the stock to cool before refrigerating. It will keep in an airtight container in the fridge for up to 5 days or in the freezer for up to 3 months. If not using rendered pork fat, skim off the fat that solidifies on the surface of the stock and add it to your shio broth.

To make the tare, place the salt in a bowl, pour over the boiling water and whisk until dissolved. Add the remaining ingredients and whisk to combine. The tare will keep in an airtight container in the fridge for up to 5 days.

To make the broth, combine all the ingredients in a saucepan and bring to a simmer, whisking.

Serve over ramen noodles with your favourite toppings.

SHOYU BROTH

800 ml (27 fl oz),
Chicken, vegetable and
fish stock

1 × quantity Shoyu tare

1½ tbsp Rendered pork
fat (see page 129) or
chicken fat

CHICKEN, VEGETABLE
AND FISH STOCK

Makes 2 litres (2 quarts)

1 kg (2 lb 3 oz) chicken
wings

1 kg (2 lb 3 oz) chicken
necks

2 onions, quartered

1 carrot, quartered

1 leek, quartered

4 dried shiitake
mushrooms

6 garlic cloves, smashed

1 tsp black peppercorns

15 g (½ oz) bonito flakes

SHOYU TARE

70 ml (2¼ fl oz) soy
sauce

3 tsp Dashi
(see page 136)

1½ tsp sake

1½ tsp mirin

1½ tsp toasted sesame
oil

¼ tsp finely grated ginger

⅓ tsp finely grated garlic

To make the stock, place the chicken wings and necks, vegetables, garlic and peppercorns in a large stockpot and cover with 5 litres (5¼ quarts) of water. Bring to the boil and skim off any impurities that rise to the surface. Reduce the heat, cover and simmer for 2–2½ hours until you are left with about 2 litres (2 quarts) of stock. Add the bonito flakes, simmer for 5 minutes, then remove from the heat.

Strain the stock and discard the solids.

Leave to cool before refrigerating. The stock will keep in an airtight container in the fridge for up to 5 days or in the freezer for up to 3 months.

To make the tare, whisk the ingredients in a small bowl to combine. The tare will keep in an airtight container in the fridge for up to 1 week.

To make the broth, combine all the ingredients in a saucepan and bring to a simmer, whisking.

Serve over ramen noodles with your favourite toppings.

TONKOTSU BROTH

MAKES 2 PORTIONS

800 ml (27 fl oz) Tonkotsu stock

1 × quantity Tonkotsu tare

1½ tbsp Rendered pork fat (see page 129)

TONKOTSU STOCK

Makes 2 litres (2 quarts)

2 kg (4 lb 6 oz) pork thigh bones, sawn into 3 cm (1¼ in) discs by your butcher

2 pig's trotters, sawn in half by your butcher

1 onion, quartered

8 garlic cloves, smashed

TONKOTSU TARE

2 tbsp Rendered Pork Fat (see page 129)

1½ tbsp tahini

2 tsp soy sauce or chashu cooking liquid (see page 128)

1 tsp mirin

1½ tsp sea salt

⅛ tsp ground white pepper

2 garlic cloves, finely grated

To make the stock, place the thigh bones and trotters, onion and garlic in a large stockpot and cover with 5 litres (5¼ quarts) of water. Bring to the boil and skim off any impurities that rise to the surface. Reduce the heat, cover and simmer for 2–2½ hours until you are left with about 2 litres (2 quarts) of stock. Remove from the heat.

Strain the stock and discard the solids.

Leave to cool before refrigerating. The stock will keep in an airtight container in the fridge for up to 5 days or in the freezer for up to 3 months.

To make the tare, whisk the ingredients in a small bowl to combine. The tare will keep in an airtight container in the fridge for up to 1 week.

To make the broth, combine all the ingredients in a saucepan and bring to a simmer, whisking.

Serve over ramen noodles with your favourite toppings.

ANCHOVY AND KELP STOCK

DASHIMA MYEOLCHI YUKSU

MAKES 1.5 LITRES (1½ QUARTS)

10 g (¼ oz) kombu (about 5–6 small pieces)

30 g (1 oz) medium dried anchovies (about 20)

Place the kombu in a large saucepan with the anchovies. Add 1.5 litres (6 cups) of water and bring to a rolling boil over high heat. Reduce the heat to medium–low and simmer for 10 minutes. Remove the konbu and discard it to prevent the stock becoming too salty. Simmer the anchovies for a further 10 minutes, then drain through a fine-mesh sieve into a clean saucepan. Discard the anchovies.

INDEX

Published in 2023 by Smith Street Books
Naarm (Melbourne) | Australia
smithstreetbooks.com

ISBN: 978-1-9227-5422-6

Publisher: Paul McNally
Editor and text: Avery Hayes
Design concept: George Saad
Design layout: Megan Ellis
Photographer: Emily Weaving
Stylist: Bridget Wald
Food preparation: Caroline Griffiths, Jane O'Shannessy
& Charlie Watts
Proofreader: Pam Dunne
Indexer: Helena Holmgren

Printed & bound in China by C&C Offset Printing Co., Ltd.

Book 256
10 9 8 7 6 5 4 3 2

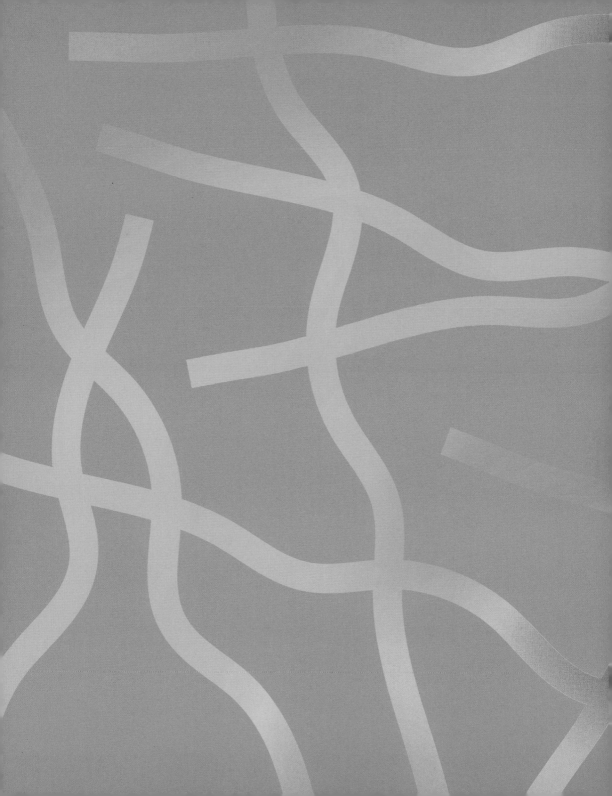